got e 9

SU...
1

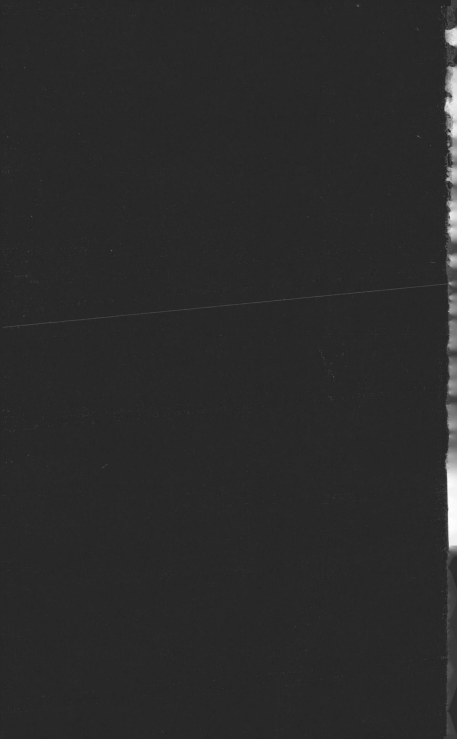

heartbreak

BOOKS BY ANDREA DWORKIN

Woman Hating
Our Blood: Prophecies and Discourses on Sexual Politics
the new woman's broken heart: short stories
Pornography: Men Possessing Women
Right-wing Women
Ice and Fire
Intercourse
Pornography and Civil Rights: A New Day for Women's Equality
  (with Catharine A. MacKinnon)
Letters from a War Zone
Mercy
Life and Death: Unapologetic Writings
On the Continuing War Against Women
In Harm's Way: The Pornography Civil Rights Hearings
  (with Catharine A. MacKinnon)
Scapegoat: The Jews, Israel, and Women's Liberation

Andrea Dworkin

heartbreak

The Political Memoir of a Feminist Militant

continuum

Continuum
The Tower Building
11 York Road
London SE1 7NX

www.continuumbooks.com

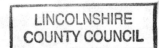

This edition first published 2006 in the UK by Continuum

British Library Cataloguing-in-Publication Data
A catalogue record for this book is available from the British Library.

ISBN 0–8264–9147–2

Typeset by Continuum
Printed and bound by MPG Books Ltd, Cornwall

*To Ricki Abrams and
Catharine A. MacKinnon*

To Ruth and Jackie

Je est un autre
Rimbaud

Contents

Preface

I have been asked, politely and not so politely, why I am myself. This is an accounting any woman will be called on to give if she asserts her will. In the home the question will be couched in a million cruelties, some subtle, some so egregious they rival the injuries of organized war.

A woman writer makes herself conspicuous by publishing, not by writing. Although one could argue – and I would – that publishing is essential to the development of the writing itself, there will be exceptions. After all, suppose Max Brod had burned Kafka's work as Kafka had wanted? The private writer, which Kafka was, must be more common among women than men: few men have Kafka's stunning self-loathing, but many women do; then again, there is the obvious – that the public domain in which the published work lives has been considered the male domain. In our day, more women publish but many more do not, and despite the glut of mediocre and worthless books published each year just in the United States, there must be a she-Kafka, or more than one, in hiding somewhere, just as there must be a she-Proust, whose vanity turned robust when it came to working over so many years on essentially one great book. If the she-Proust were lucky enough to live long enough and could afford the rewards of a purely aesthetic life, aggressive self-publication and promotion would not necessarily follow: her secret masterpiece would be just that – secret, yet no less a masterpiece. The tree fell; no one heard it or ever will; it exists.

In our day, a published woman's reputation, if she is alive, will depend on many small conformities – in her writing but especially in her life. Does she practice the expression of gender in a good way, which is to say, does she convince, in her person, that she is female down to the very marrow of her bones? Her supplications may be modest, but most often they are not. Her lips will blaze red even if she is old and gnarled. It's a declaration: I won't hurt you; I am deferential; all those unpleasant things I said, I didn't mean one of them. In our benumbed era, which tries for a semblance of civilized, voluntary order after the morbid, systematic chaos of Hitler, Stalin, and Mao – after Pol Pot and the unspeakable starving of Africa – it is up to women, as it always has been, to embody the meaning of civilized life on the scale of one to one, each of those matchings containing within and underneath rivers running with a historical blood. Women in Western societies now take the following loyalty oath: my veil was made by Revlon, and I will not show my face; I believe in free speech, which includes the buying and selling of my sisters in pornography and prostitution, but if we call it "trafficking," I'm agin it –

how dare one exploit Third World or foreign or exotic women; my body is mostly skeleton and if anyone wants to write on it, they must use the finest brush and write the simplest of haiku; I have sex, I like sex, I am sex, and while being used may offend me on principle or concretely, I will fight back by manipulation and lies but deny it from kindergarten to the grave; I have no sense of honor and, girls, if there's one thing you can count on, you can count on that. If this were not the common, current practice – if triviality and deceit were not the coin of the female realm – there would be nothing remarkable in who I am or how I got the way that I am.

It must be admitted that those who want me to account for myself are intrigued in hostile, voyeuristic ways, and their projections of me are not the usual run-of-the-mill rudeness or arrogance to which writers, especially women writers, become accustomed. The work would be enough, even for the unfortunate sad sacks mentioned above. So here's the deal as I see it: I am ambitious – God knows, not for money; in most respects but not all I am honorable; and I wear overalls: kill the bitch. But the bitch is not yet ready to die. Brava, she says, alone in a small room.

Music 1

I studied music when I was a child, the piano as taught by Mrs. Smith. She was old with white hair. She represented culture with every gesture while I was just a plebe kid. But I learned: discipline and patience from Czerny, the way ideas can move through sound from Bach, how to say "Fuck you" from Mozart. Mrs. Smith might have thought herself the reigning sensibility, and she did get between the student and the music with a stunning regularity, but if you could hear you could learn and if you learned it in your body you knew it forever. The fingers were the wells of musical memory, and they provided a map for the cognitive faculties. I can remember writing out the notes and eventually grasping the nature of the piano, percussive and string, the richness and range of the sound. I wanted music in writing but not the way Verlaine did, not in the syllables themselves; anything pronounced would have sound and most sound is musical; no, in a different way. I recognized early on how the great classical composers, but especially and always Bach, could convey ideas without using any words at all. Repetition, variation, risk, originality, and commitment created the piece and conveyed the ideas. I wanted to do that with writing. I'd walk around with poems by Rimbaud or Baudelaire in my pocket – bilingual, paperback books with the English translations reading like prose poems – and I'd recognize that the power of the poems was not unlike the power of music. For a while, I hoped to be a pianist, and my mother took me into Philadelphia, the big city, to study with someone a great deal more pretentious and more expensive than Mrs. Smith. But then I tried to master Tchaikovsky's Piano Concerto No. 1, for which I had developed a somewhat warped passion, and could not. That failure told me that I could not be a musician, although I continued to study music in college.

The problem with that part of my musical education was that I stopped playing piano, and Bennington, the college I went to, insisted that one play an instrument. I didn't like my piano teacher, and I wasn't going to play or spend one minute of one day with him hovering over my shoulder and condemning me with a baronial English that left my prior teachers in my mind as plain-speaking people. I loved the theory classes. Mine was with the composer Vivian fine. The first assignment, which was lovely, was to write a piece for salt and pepper shakers. I wrote music away from the piano for the piano, but after the first piano lesson I never deigned to darken the piano teacher's doorway again. At the end of the year, this strategy of noncompliance turned out to be the equivalent of not attending physical education in high school: you couldn't graduate without having done the awful crap. When my adviser, also a musician but never a teacher of music to me, asked me why I hadn't shown up for any of the piano lessons, I felt awkward and stupid but I gave him an honest answer: "I don't like the asshole." My adviser smiled with one of his this-is-too-good-to-be-true looks – he was amused – and said he'd take care of it. He must have, or I would not have passed.

My adviser, the composer Louis Callabro, taught me a lot about music, but there was always a kind of cross-fertilization – I'd bring the poems, the short stories, every now and then a novel. Lou was a drunkard, much more his style than being an alcoholic. I had met him without knowing it on first arriving at Bennington. I loved the old music building and sort of haunted it. He came out of his studio, pissing drunk, stared at me, and said, "Never sleep with a man if you want to be his friend." I adored the guy. Eventually I'd show him my music and he'd show me his short stories. It was a new version of I'll-show-you-mine-if-you-show-me-yours. I later understood that the all-girl Bennington's expectation was that the girl, the woman, any female student, should learn how to be the mistress of an artist, not the artist herself: this in the college that was the early home of Martha Graham. The equality between Lou and myself, our mutual recognition, was no part of the school's agenda. This is not to suggest that Lou did not screw his students: he did; they all did. I always thought that I would go to heaven because at Bennington I never slept with faculty members, only their wives.

Music 2

Mrs. Smith used to give her students stars and points for memorizing pieces. I was used to being a good student. I got a lot of stars and a lot of points. But there was a piece I could never remember. I worked on it for months, and the denouement was in the two terrible black stars she gave me to mark my failure. The piece was *Tales from the Vienna Woods* by Strauss. I like to think that my inability to stomach that piece was a repudiation of the later Strauss's Nazi politics, even though I didn't know about the former or the latter's politics at the time (and they're not related). In the same way, there was a recurrent nightmare I had when I stayed with my mother's mother, Sadie Spiegel. The room got smaller and smaller and I had trouble breathing. The tin soldiers I associated with *Tales* were like a drum corps around the shrinking room. Later, cousins told me about their father's sexual molestation of them. Their father was Sadie's favorite, the youngest of her children; he was brilliant as well as blond and beautiful, had a role in inventing the microchip, and he stuck his penis down the throats of at least two of his children when they were very young, including when they were infants

– I assume to elicit the involuntary sucking response. Even though my cousins told me this horror years later, I like to think that reality runs like a stream, except that time isn't linear and the nightmare was a synthesis, Strauss and my uncle, Nazis both. And yes, I mean it. A man who sticks his cock in an infant's mouth belongs in Himmler's circle of hell.

Music 3

There was jazz and Bessie Smith. When I'd cut high school or college and go to Eighth Street in New York City, I'd find used albums. I listened to every jazz great I could find. My best friend in high school particularly liked Maynard Fergusson, a white jazz man. I went to hear him at the Steel Pier in Atlantic City when I was a kid. (I also went to hear Ricky Nelson at the Steel Pier. I stood among hundreds of screaming girl teens but up front. The teens who fainted, I am here to tell you, fainted from the heat of a South Jersey summer misspent in a closed ballroom. Still, I adored Ricky and Pat Boone and, special among specials, Tab Hunter with his cover of "Red Sails in the Sunset.") There was no gambling then, just miles of boardwalk with penny arcades, cotton candy, saltwater taffy, root-beer sodas in frosted-glass mugs; and sand, ocean, music. I listened to Coltrane, had a visceral love of Charlie Parker that I still have, listened to "K.C. Blues" covers wherever I could find them. When I was a teen, I also came across Billie Holiday, and her voice haunts me to this day – I can hear it in my head anytime – and with "Strange Fruit" and "God Bless the Child" she sounded more like a blues singer than a jazz woman; but the bulk of her work, which I heard later, was jazz. It was her voice that was blues. When her voice wasn't blues, it meant the heroin had dragged her way down and she couldn't go lower. "Strange Fruit" was worth anything it took from her, and so was "God Bless the Child." I'm not happy with art as necrophilia, but I think these two songs, and "Strange Fruit" in particular, were worth her life. They'd be worth mine.

My brother, Mark, and I both had a taste for the Ahmad Jamal Quartet. I loved the live jazz in the clubs, the informal jazz I found live in the apartments of various lovers, and I wanted to hear anyone I was lucky enough to hear about. I craved jazz music, and the black world was where one found it. There was a tangle of sex and jazz, black culture and black male love. There was a Gordian knot made of black men and Jewish white women in particular. Speaking only for myself, I wasn't going to settle in the suburbs, and New York City meant black, jazz meant black, blues meant black.

Philadelphia, in contrast, had folk music and coffeehouses with live performers. Most were white. I liked Dave Van Ronk and in junior high school stole an album of his from a big Philadelphia department store; or maybe it was just the bearded white face on the album cover, an archetype egging me on. My best friend in high school liked the Philly scene with its scuzzy, mostly failed musicians and its folk music. I'd go with her when I could because Philly promised excitement, though it rarely delivered. She and I flirted with a small Bohemia, not life-threatening, whereas when I was alone in New York City there was no net. In the environs of Philly I went to hear Joan Baez, whose voice was splendid, and I listened to folk music on record, Baez, Buffy Sainte-Marie, and Ramblin' Jack Eliot, who rambled in those days mostly in Philadelphia. These took me back to Woody Guthrie, Leadbelly, and Cisco Houston. By the time Bob Dylan came along, I was uninterested in the genre altogether until some friends in college made me sit down to listen to Dylan *soi-même*. Even then, it was his politics that moved me, not his music. That changed. It changed the first time because he was an acquired taste, and after listening enough I acquired sufficient love of the music-with-lyric to be one with my generation; and it changed the second time, years later, maybe decades later, when his marriage fell apart and I found out that he had been a batterer. He lost me. I can't claim any purity on this, because I've never lost my taste for Miles Davis, and he was a really bad guy to women, including through battery. So I love ol' Miles, but I sure do have trouble putting any CD of his in the machine. In Amsterdam I met Ben Webster, but so did any white girl. He was way past his prime, but he still played his heart out. I remember the saliva dripping from his lips and the sweat that blanketed his fat body or the visible parts of it. He'd sit in the sun in Leidseplein; he always wore a suit; and he'd be the Pied Piper. I wished he had been Fats Waller, whom I've rediscovered on CD. I heard B. B. King in concert a few times there, and the Band once. I loved B. B., whom I met years later, and I loved the Band.

But it was Bessie who came to stand for art in my mind. I found her albums, three for 33 cents, in a bin on Eighth Street while I was in high school, and once I listened to her I was never the same. I don't mean her kick-ass lyrics, though those are pretty much the only blues lyrics I can still stomach. I mean her stance. She had attitude on every level and at the same time a cold artistry, entirely unsentimental. Her detachment equaled her commitment: she was going to sing the song through your corporeality. Unlike smoke, which circled the body, her song went right through you, and either you took what you could get of it for the moment the note was moving inside you or she wasn't for you and you were a barrier she penetrated. Any song she sang was a second-by-second lesson in the meaning of mortality. The notes came from her and tramped through your three-dimensional body but gracefully, a spartan, bearlike ballet. I listened to those three albums hundreds of times, and each time I learned more about what art took from you to make: not love but art.

Before the compact-disc revolution, you couldn't get good or even passable albums by Ma Rainey, so she was a taste deferred, and the brilliant Alberta Hunter came into my life when I was in college and she was singing at the Cookery in New York City, a very old black woman with a pianist as her sole accompaniment. I would have done pretty much anything to hear Big Mama Thornton live, and, of course, for me, college-aged, Janis Joplin was the top, the best, the risk-taker, the one who left blood on the stage. When I lived on Crete, still college-aged, Elvis won me with "Heartbreak Hotel." Even now I can't hear it without the winds from the Aegean blowing right by me. But when it comes to conveying ideas without words, jazz triumphs. A U.S. writer without jazz and blues in her veins must have ice water instead.

The Pedophilic Teacher

I was lucky enough to have three brilliant teachers in junior high and high school. The first, in junior high, was Mr. Smith, who was a political conservative at a time when the word was not in common usage and not many people, including me, knew what it meant. He taught English, especially how to parse and diagram sentences, over and over, so that the structure of the language became embedded in one's brain and was like gravity – no personal concern yet omnipresent. You could run your fingers through English the way God could run his fingers through your hair. He was the Czerny of grammar.

The second was Mr. Belfield, who taught honors American history. I had him for two years, the eleventh and twelfth grades. Very little at Bennington later was as interesting or as demanding. He had unspeakably high standards, as befitted someone who had wanted to be secretary of state. It was wonderful not to be condescended to; not to be simply passing time; not to waste the hours waiting for some minor diversion to make one alert; to have one's own intellect stretched until it was about ready to break. He too was a political conservative and seemed to live a solitary, affectionless life. But then, I wouldn't know, would I? And that is exactly right. There is no reason for any student to know. The line separating student and teacher needs to be drawn, and it's up to the teacher to do it. The combination of Mr. Belfield's own intellectual rigor and his substantive demands were a total blessing: he taught me how to write a book. I worked hard in his class, and I cannot think of any other teacher who was so authentic and committed, whose pedagogy was disinterested in the best sense, not a toying with the minds of students nor fucking with their aspirations for better or worse: he wanted heroic work – he demanded it. You might say that he was the Wagner of American history without the loathsome anti-Semitism and misshapen ego. Other people accused him of arrogance, but I thought he was humble – he was modest to use his gifts to teach us. Neither Mr. Smith nor Mr. Belfield ever allowed the deep sleep of mediocrity; neither wanted narcoleptic students; you couldn't play either of them for favors, and they didn't play you.

The third great teacher was different in substance and in kind. He liked little girls, especially little Jewish girls. I don't mean five-year-olds, although maybe he liked them too. But he liked us, my two best friends and me. He had sexualized relationships with the three of us. He played us against each other: Who was going to get him at the end of the day or through his machinations get to skip a class to see him? Who had spent the most time with him that day? Who had had the sexiest conversation with him? I thought that he and I were going to found a school of philosophy together; he would be the leader and I would be his acolyte. The sexiest thing about him was the range of his experience, not only concerning sex. He knew jazz; he introduced me to Sartre and Camus, though not de Beauvoir, certainly not; he had smoked marijuana and talked about it; he encouraged identification with bad-boy, alienated Holden Caulfield and through Holden the wretched Franny and Zooey; he drew me pictures of all the sex acts, including oral and anal sex; he printed by hand the names of the acts and instructed me in how to pursue men, not boys; he suggested to me that I become a prostitute – as he put it, it was more interesting than becoming a hairdresser, which was the one profession in his view open to women of my social class; he encouraged disobedience in general and affirmed that I was right to be so disenchanted with and contemptuous of the pukey adults who were my other teachers and to hate and defy all their stupid rules. At the same time, he was very controlling: my friends and I danced his dance; he partnered each of us and all of us; he created configurations of sex and love that manipulated, sexualized, and intensified our friendships with each other – it was a *ménage à quatre*; he knew what each of us wanted and there he was dangling it and if you were part of his sexual delight he'd give you a taste.

We thought that he was the one honest one, the one hip one. He knew who Jack Kerouac and Allen Ginsberg were; where Tangiers was; the oeuvre of Henry Miller and of Lawrence Durrell; what the politics of the Algerian War were, especially as it related to Camus; in fact he had actually been to Paris; he knew that sometimes, like Socrates, you needed to swallow the poison and other times, like Che, you needed to use the barrel of a gun. In other words, he was dazzling. He was the world outside the prison walls, and escape was my sole desire.

His best trick was giving the three of us passes to get us out of classes we didn't like, and we'd get to spend that time with him learning real stuff: sex stuff or sexy stuff. For instance, instead of the traditional candy bar, he offered me written excuses from my mathematics classes, time better spent with him: it's a wonder I can count to one. He fucked one of us on graduation night and kept up an emotionally abusive relationship with her for years. I almost committed suicide at sixteen because I didn't think he loved me, though he later assured me that he did in a hot and heavy phone call: under his influence and Salinger's I had walked out into the ocean prepared to drown. The waves got up to about chest level when I realized that the water was fucking cold, and I turned myself around and got right out of that big, old ocean, though the ocean itself, not suicide, continues to entrance me. In my heart from then to this day, I became antisuicide; it took me longer – far too long – to become antipedophilic.

I thought Paul Goodman was right when he wrote in *Growing Up Absurd* that sex had always been passed on from adults to children; college-aged, I met Goodman, watched and experienced some of his cruelty to women, and was bewildered, though I knew I didn't like the cruelty and I didn't like him. How could someone write a rebel's book and be so mean? To me, that was a formidable mystery. In later years my friend Judith Malina, who directed a play of Goodman's though he taunted her repeatedly by saying women could not direct, told me about how he slapped her during a therapy session – he was the therapist. Of course, Goodman was a pedophile and a misogynist, as was Allen Ginsberg, whom I met later. I say "of course" because there is a specific kind of education the pedophilic teacher gives: the education itself is a seduction, a long, exciting-but-drawn-out coupling, an intellectually dishonest, soul-rending passion in which the curiosity and adventuresomeness of the younger person is used as the hook, a cynical use because the younger person needs what the older provides. It may be attention or a sense of importance or knowledge denied her or him by other adults. In my case I was Little Eva, and a snake offered knowledge and the promise of escape from the constriction of a dead world in which there were no poets or geniuses or visionaries. All the girls, after all, were expected to teach, nurse, do hair, or clean houses, or combinations as if from a Chinese menu. Because most adults lie to children most of the time, the pedophilic adult seems to be a truth-teller, the one adult ready and willing to know the world and not to lie about it. Lordy, lordy, I do still love that piece of shit.

"Silent Night"

It was the sixth grade, I was ten, we had just moved from Camden to the suburbs, and I wouldn't sing it: that simple. They put me alone in a big, empty classroom and let me sweat it out for a while. Then they sent in a turncoat Jew, a pretty, gutless teacher, who said that she was Jewish and she sang "Silent Night" so why didn't I? It was my first experience with a female collaborator, or the first one that I remember. They left me alone in the empty classroom after that. I wasn't a religious zealot; I just didn't like being pushed around, and I knew about and liked the separation of church and state, and I knew I wasn't a Christian and I didn't worship Jesus. I even knew that Christians had made something of a habit of killing Jews, which sealed the deal for me. I was shunned, and one of my drawings, hung in the hall on a bulletin board, was defaced: "kike" was written across it. I then had to undergo the excruciating process of getting some adult to tell me what "kike" meant. I thought my teachers were fascists in the style of the Inquisition for wanting me to sing "Silent Night" when they knew I was Jewish, and I still think that. What they take from you in school is eroded slowly, but this was big. I couldn't understand how they could try to force me. Transparently, they could and they did. Force, punishment, exile: so much adult firepower to use against such a little girl. To this day I think about this confrontation with authority as the "Silent Night" Action, and I recommend it. Adults need to be stood up to by children, period. It's good for them, the adults, I mean. Pushing kids around is ugly. The adults need to be saved from themselves. On the other hand, students should not, must not shoot teachers. The nobility of rebellion student-to-teacher requires civil disobedience, not guns, not war – pedagogy against pedagogy. In this context, guns are cowardly.

I was, however, in crisis. I had read *Gone with the Wind* probably a hundred times, and like Scarlett I was willful. My problem was the following: abortion was illegal and women were dying. How could this be changed? Was the best way to write a book that made you cry your heart out and feel the suffering of the sick and dying women or to go into court à la Perry Mason and make an argument so compelling, so truthful and poignant, that people would rise up unable to bear the pain of the status quo? You might say that in some sense I was fully formed in the sixth grade. My frame of reference was not expansive – I did not yet know about Danton or Robespierre or any number of referent points beside Perry Mason – but in formal terms the dilemma of my life was fully present: law or literature, literature or law? By the end of that year, I had decided that they could stop you from going to law school –

and would – but no one could keep you from writing because nobody had to know about it.

It was my mother whose politics were represented by the abortion theme: she supported legal birth control and legal abortion long before these were respectable beliefs. I had learned these prowoman political positions from her, and I think of her every time I fight for a woman's reproductive rights or write a check to the National Abortion Rights Action League or Planned Parenthood. Our arguments for the abortion right now might be more politically sophisticated, but my mother had the heart and politics of a pioneer – only I didn't understand that. These were the reproductive politics I grew up with, and so I did not know that she had taught me what I presumed was fair and right.

Eventually she would tell me that the worst mistake she had made in raising me was in teaching me how to read; she had a mordant sense of humor that she rarely exercised. The public library in the newly hatched suburb of Delaware Township, later to become Cherry Hill, was in the police station or next door to it; and my mother found herself writing notes giving me permission to take out *Lolita* or *Peyton Place*. To her credit she did write those notes each and every time I wanted to read a book that was forbidden for children. Or I think it's to her credit. I don't know why later she would not let me see the film *A Summer Place* with Sandra Dee and Troy Donahue (the two are teenaged lovers and Sandra gets pregnant) when I had already read the book. We had a screaming match that lasted several days. She won, of course. It was the sheer exercise of parental authority that gave her the victory, and I despised her for not being able to win the argument on the merits. She'd blow up at my curiosity or precociousness, and it seemed to come out of nowhere to me. What she hated wasn't what I read or the movies I saw but what I started writing, because sixth grade was the beginning of writing my own poems. They'd be small and imitative, but they were piss-perfect, in-your-face acts of rebellion. The adults could keep lying, but I wouldn't. My mother's real failure was in telling me not to lie. I had a literalist sense of the meaning of the admonition. I was a "kike" and would continue to be one: never once have I sung "Silent Night" nor will I. I recognized that there were a lot of ways of lying, and pretending that Christmas and Easter were secular holidays was a big lie, not a small one. Whether the issue was segregation or abortion, I, the sixth-grader, was going to deal with it, and my vehicle was going to be truth: not a global, self-deluded truth, not a truth that only I knew and that I wanted other people to follow, but the truth that came from not lying. Like "do no harm," not lying is a big one, a hard discipline, a practice of spartan ethics too often mistaken for self-righteousness. If putting my body there when it ought to be here was required but to do so was to lie, I wasn't going to do it. I'd write and I wouldn't lie. So when self-help writers tell one to find the child within, I assume they don't mean me.

Plato

A girl is faced with hard decisions. What is written inside those decisions is inscrutable to her; by necessity – her age, time, place, sex discrimination in general – she sees or knows only the surfaces. So in junior high school I was thrilled when I was allowed to wear lipstick for the first time, a rite of passage that has nothing to do with sexuality but everything to do with maturity, becoming an adult fast and easy. My first lipstick was called Tangerine, and like other girls I spent hours thinking about what it went with, what it meant, and how my life was finally beginning to cohere. It was also the first recognition from my mother – all-important, the whole deal has little to do with men or boys at all – that I was nearly adult but certainly no child.

I'd wear Tangerine, along with a favorite dress that let me see my own breasts, a deep V-neck, a cut I still like, and I'd be making my way through Plato's *Symposium*. It had been communicated to me through the odd, secret whispers of women that a female's nose must never shine. In war, in famine, in fire, it had to be matte, and no one got a lipstick without the requisite face powder. On my own I added my own favorite, Erase, which went over the powder (or was it under?) and got the lines under your eyes to disappear. In this way I could hide my late-night reading from my parents – circles under the eyes were a dead giveaway. I would pretend to go to sleep; I'd wait for them to go to sleep; I'd turn on my reading light, read, and simultaneously listen for any movement at their end of the house, at which point I'd get rid of any light in my room, hide the book, and wait until I heard my mother or father return to their bed.

I was taunted by this problem: how could someone write something like the *Symposium* and make sure that her nose did not shine at the same time? It didn't matter to me that I was reading a translation. I'd read Plato's brilliant, dense prose and not be able to tear myself away. Even as a reader my nose shined. It was clearly either/or. You had to concentrate on either one or the other. In a New York minute, the oil from Saudi Arabia could infiltrate your house and end up on your nose. It didn't hurt, it didn't make noise, it didn't incapacitate in any way except for the fact that no girl worth her salt took enough time away from vigilance to read a book let alone write one. Plato was my idea of a paperback writer: the Beatles were not yet on the horizon, and anyway I'm sure that John would have agreed with me. There was nothing I wanted so much in life as to write the way Plato wrote: words inside ideas inside words, the calzone approach attenuated with Bach. I'd look at my cheap Modigliani reproductions or the reproduced females by

Rodin or Manet, and I didn't see the shine, except for that of the paper itself; but more to the point, in no book about the artists themselves that I could find was the problem of the shine addressed. These were the kind of girl-things that pre-occupied me.

Or, for instance, when it came to lying: in elementary school one would play checkers with the boys. My mother had said don't lie and had also told me that I had to lose at games to the boys if I wanted them to like me. These were irreconcilable opposites. It was, first of all, virtually impossible to lose to the boys in an honest game of checkers. Second, who wanted to? Third, how would I ever respect him or them in the morning? It did strike me that the boys you had to lose to weren't worth having, but my argument made no impression on my mother nor on anyone else I was ever to meet until the women's movement. And it was damned hard to lose at checkers to the pimply or prepimply dolts. I now think of the having-to-lose part as SWAT-team training in strategy, how to lose being harder than how to win. It was hideous for a girl to be brazenly out for the kill or to enjoy the status of victor or to enjoy her own intelligence and its application in real time.

I still remember how in the eighth or ninth grade Miss Fox, one of my nemeses among English teachers, made us skip the first three pages of *Romeo and Juliet* – the part about the maiden-heads – only to read aloud Juliet herself throughout the rest of the play, partnered with the captain of the football team as Romeo. Stereotypes aside, his reading was not delightful. And yet we all had to sit there and wait while he tried manfully, as it were, to sound out words. Her pedagogy was to encourage him while letting the rest of us rot.

I, true to form, wanted to know what a maidenhead was, and to say that I was relentless on the subject would be to understate. Miss Fox's retaliation was authoritarian and extreme. I had been out of class sick and had to take a makeup vocabulary test, multiple choice. I failed. I did not just fail: I got a zero. I was pained but respectful on my first five or ten trips up to her desk to ask her how it was possible to get a zero on a multiple-choice test, even if one did not know the meaning of one word on the test. Finally, exhausted, I just asked her to regrade the test. Since she was sure of her rightness in all things English, we struck a deal: she'd regrade the test and whatever the outcome I'd shut up. She glistened with superiority, Eve the second after biting into the apple; I was tense now that the challenge had been taken up. It turned out that she had used the wrong key in grading the test; the answers she wanted me to give were for some other test. I was good but not that good. I wanted out, Tangerine lipstick notwithstanding. I wanted smart people whether or not their noses shined enough to illuminate a room or a house or a city. I wanted someone who cared about me in particular, as an individual, enough to notice that I could not get a zero on a vocabulary test because

I had too big a vocabulary. I was so worn out by Miss Fox that when she graded an essay on contemporary education a B because, as she said to me, some commas were wrong and it wasn't anything personal, after a halfhearted and utterly futile argument I accepted the B. She even put her arm around me, genuinely adding insult to injury. I knew I'd get her someday and this is it: eat shit, bitch. No one said that sisterhood was easy.

The High School Library

Nowadays librarians actively try to get students Internet access to pornography, at least in the United States. Organized as a First Amendment lobby group, librarians go to court – or their professional organizations do – to defend pornographers and pornography. Truly, this does not happen because James Joyce and Henry Miller were banned as obscene a hundred years ago; I once wrote an affidavit for a court on the differences between Nabokov's *Lolita* and a pimp's pictorial with words, "Lolita Pissing." These are some of life's easier distinctions. I used to ask groups of folks how the retailers of pornography could tell the difference between Joyce and hard-core visual pornography. I noted that although, generally speaking, they weren't the best and the brightest, they managed never to stock *Ulysses*. If they could do it, I thought, so could the rest of us. Instead, the idea seems to be that keeping a child – someone underaged – away from anything is akin to treason. One is violating sacred constitutional rights and assassinating Jefferson, Washington, and Lincoln (for the second time).

In my high school days, librarians were the militia, the first line of defense in keeping the underaged away from books, all sorts of books in every field.

My high school library was tall, I remember, as if piles of books held up the ceiling; it was dense with books organized according to the Dewey decimal system. I liked to look at and to touch the books. I believed I could feel the heat emanating from them, and no heat meant no light. My father had told me I had to read everything, that to read books of only one view was the equivalent of a moral wrong. When I asked why, he uttered the incomprehensible words: "Sometimes writers lie." In my early years, my parents made up for the latitude they gave me in reading by seeing to it that I read on a continuum, both political and literary. When I went weak in the knees for Dostoyevsky, my dad gave me some Mark Twain or my mother one of Eric Bentley's books on the theater. I just wanted to read everything; there was never enough. It wasn't quite as simple as it sounds. My mother was more tense about what I read than my father, but then, she was in the thick of it: my bad attitudes, bad habits, and bad behavior. I did get ideas from books: that's what they're for. I've been astonished by the pro-pornography argument that people are not influenced by what they read or see. Why, then, bother writing or making films? One wants to persuade. One wants to knock the reader senseless with the shock of the new or the old reconceived. Rimbaud articulated the writing ambition when he wanted to derange the senses, though he meant his own. Sometimes it's the rawness of the writing that makes everything inside shake and break; sometimes it's the delicacy of the writing that makes everything inside simply recognize a reality different from the known one or experience a lyricism heretofore unknown. For me, subtle writing was almost always anti-urban; it took me to the steppes of Russia or Huck Finn's South.

The library brought the world to me: I went with Darwin on the HMS *Beagle* and I dived with Freud into the mind and I plotted with Marx about how to end poverty. I had read most of Freud, all of Darwin, and most of Marx before I graduated from high school. This was not with the help of the high school librarians.

Instead, I learned their work schedules, because we were not allowed to take out more than two books a day and I needed a bigger fix than that. All records were kept by hand. So if I went into the library during a new shift, I could get two more books, then two more, then two more. The librarians treated the books like contraband, and so did I. My friends and I had a commitment to *Catcher in the Rye*, which was not allowed in the library. We bought a lot of copies over time. We shelved them. Each time it would be a different one of us who had the responsibility for getting the book into the library, on the shelves. Sometimes we catalogued the book – what was gained if no one knew it was there? – and other times we shelved it as if it were plastique. Eventually the head librarian would find it; we'd know by the dirty looks we got from her long before we got to check on the book itself.

Catcher was a rallying point for our high school intelligentsia. I remember going to my parents for help: I asked if they would fight with the school board to get the book in the library. They would not. I found this refusal confusing, an abrogation of everything they had taught me. Actually it outraged me. One of my friends had his editorial removed from the school paper because it was about the wrongness of banning *Catcher* from the high school library. So we fought on, invisible guardians of one orphan book.

Then one day it happened: the school board took things in hand themselves. They went through the library to get rid of all socialistic, communistic, anti-God books. Surveying the damage when they had finished, I saw no Eugene V. Debs or Norman Thomas, certainly no Darwin, Freud, or Marx; but one slim volume called *Guerrilla Warfare* by a person named Che Guevara had escaped the purge. I was bound for life to the man. I studied that book the way the Chinese were forced to study Chairman Mao. I planned revolutionary attacks on the local shopping mall. We had a paucity of mountains in the suburbs, so it was hard to apply many of Che's strategic points; the land was flat, flat, flat; the mall – the first in the country – was boring, boring, boring, emphatically not Havana. I studied Che's principles of revolution day in and day out, and the school board was none the wiser. The shelves in the library now were roomy, and the room itself seemed lower. There weren't books in piles to hold up the ceiling, nor were there books that emanated heat and with the heat enough light to be a candle in the darkness. It was as if anything the school board recognized it did away with. I was almost out. My term of imprisonment was almost up. My own hard time was coming to an end. The pedophilic teacher had a lot of anger and despair to fool around with, and he didn't let any of it go to waste. He'd tell you any story you wanted to hear, give you the narrative of any book gone missing; *Anna Karenina* went from being Tolstoy's to being his.

The Bookstore

Sometime during high school the very best thing happened: at the mall a bookstore opened. This was a spectacular bookstore, independent, few hardcover books but they were out of my socioeconomic league anyway; and there was a whole rack of City Lights books, yes, Ginsberg and Ferlinghetti and Robert Duncan and Paul Blackburn and Gregory Corso and Yevteshenko – anything City Lights published would show up on that rack. It was all contemporary, all poetry, all incendiary, all revolutionary, each book a Molotov cocktail. I'd be down and the owners would point me to something, and I'd be up and they'd point me to something else. It was a whole world of books that I never dreamed could be so close to me, to where I was physically on the planet: this horrible, awful, stupid suburb. The store was owned and run by two adults, Stan and Phyllis Pogran, who were not trying to get between you and the books; they brought you right to the trough and let you drink. You could read the books in the store (there were no chairs in bookstores back then); you didn't have to buy and I rarely could, although any money I had went to buy books or music, which is still the case. I had never met adults like Stan and Phyllis. Later they separated and divorced, but I swear they kept me alive and kicking: I never had a mood I couldn't find on their shelves.

There was never a book they tried to hide from you. At the same time, they weren't trying to use you – you weren't the day's kick for them; they were the opposite of the pedophilic teacher. They let me talk to them about books and about being a writer and they talked right back about books and writing. Amid the vulgarity of the shopping mall, with its caged birds and fountains, its gushing-over department stores and restaurants, there was this one island of insanity, since the rest passed for normal. You could get close to any poet you wanted and they, the booksellers, didn't enforce the law on you: they didn't bayonet your guts until all the poetry had spilled out, all the desire for poetry had been bled to death, all the music in your heart had been lanced, all your dreams trounced on and ripped to pieces. I found James Baldwin there and read everything he had written; I breathed with him. I found Mailer and Gore Vidal. I found Tennessee Williams and Edward Albee. I'd walk over from my house in any spare time I had – "I'm going to the mall, Ma" had its own legitimacy, a reassuring, implicit conformity – and I'd haunt the shelves and I'd find the world outside the world in which I was living. I'd find a world of beauty and ideas. Corso liked Shelley, so I read Shelley and from him Byron and Keats. I read Joyce and Miller and Homer and Euripides and Hemingway and

Fitzgerald and Gertrude Stein. They were all there, in this one tiny bookstore, and my love affair with books became a wild and long ride, bucking bronco after bucking bronco; I found Genet and Burroughs; I read *The Blacks* and *Naked Lunch*. Literature exploded. I found and read the early pirated edition of *The Story of O*.

The only bad part was that I couldn't live there, sleep in a corner resting my head on a messed-up coat; the store would close and I had to go home. By the next day I'd barely be able to breathe from the thrill of knowing I was going to find a way to get back to the bookstore and find another book and one after that, another author and one after that.

It would be a few years before the feminist ferment would begin to produce a renaissance of luminous and groundbreaking books; and *Sexual Politics* by Kate Millett did change my life. I was one of the ones it was written for, because I had absorbed the writers she exposed, I had believed in them; in the euphoria of finding what I thought were truth-tellers, I had forgotten my father's warning that some writers lie. But still, one doesn't know what one doesn't know, even Mailer, even Albee. It's not as if there's an empty patch that one can see and so one can say, "There's my ignorance; it's about ten by ten and a dozen feet high and someday someone will fill in the empty patch and I'll find what I need, what I must know in order to lead a full and honorable life." These writers, Stein excepted, did not acknowledge women as other than subhuman monsters of sex and predation; and their prose and chutzpah made me a fellow traveler. All one can do is to fight illegitimate authority, expressed in my world by adults, and find a church. Books were my church but even more my native land, my place of refuge, my DP camp. I was an exile early on, but exile welcomed me; it was where I belonged.

The Fight

I loved Allen Ginsberg with the passion that only a teenager knows, but that passion did not end when adolescence did. I sent him poems when I was in high school and barely breathed until I heard back from him. He critiqued the poems I sent on a postcard that I got about three weeks later, though it seemed like ten years. I thought I would die – he acknowledged me as if I were a writer and we lived in the same world. In college I went to every reading of his that I could. My heart breathed with his, or so I thought, but I was too shy ever to introduce myself to him or hang around him until the one reading after which I did introduce myself. "Call me," he said to me a half dozen times as I was walking backward out of the large room, backward so that he could keep talking to me. "Call me," he had said, "but don't come to New York just to call me or you'll drive me mad." He had scribbled his phone number on a piece of paper. "Call me," he repeated over and over. I could have happily died then and there.

I did go to New York just to see him, but when I got to New York I was too shy to call him. I'd spend every waking hour worrying about how to make the call. I picked a rainy night. He answered the phone. "Come on over now," he said. I told him that he was much too busy. I told him that it was raining. I went anyway, shaking on the wet sidewalks, shaking on the bus, so nervous on the five flights up to his apartment that I could barely keep my balance. As always when I was nervous, I broke into a cold sweat.

He had warned me that he was working on proofs for a new book of poems and would have very little time for me, but we spent the whole night talking – well, okay, not all of it but many hours of it. He then walked me down to the bus in the rain and told me he loved me. I counted. He told me eleven times.

I called him one more time many months later. I had a standing invitation to see him, but I never went back. I stayed infatuated but I stayed out of his way. I did not know that this was a shrewd move on my part for the writer I wanted to be. Being in thrall to an icon keeps you from becoming yourself.

When *Woman Hating* was published in 1974, I met the photographer Elsa Dorfman. She was a close friend of Allen's and had photographed him and other writers over years, not days. She photographed me for the first time as a writer. When Elsa had a baby I was asked to be his godmother and Ginsberg was his godfather. We were now, metaphysically speaking, joined in unholy matrimony. And still I stayed away from him. I did not see him again, since that time in college, until my godson was bar mitzvahed. By this time I had published many books, including my work attacking pornography – the artifacts, the philosophy, the politics.

On the day of the bar mitzvah newspapers reported in huge headlines that the Supreme Court had ruled child pornography illegal. I was thrilled. I knew that Allen would not be. I did think he was a civil libertarian. But in fact, he was a pedophile. He did not belong to the North American Man-Boy Love Association out of some mad, abstract conviction that its voice had to be heard. He meant it. I take this from what Allen said directly to me, not from some inference I made. He was exceptionally aggressive about his right to fuck children and his constant pursuit of underage boys.

I did everything I could to avoid Allen and to avoid conflict. This was my godson's day. He did not need a political struggle to the death breaking out all over.

Ginsberg would not leave me alone. He followed me everywhere I went from the lobby of the hotel through the whole reception, then during the dinner. He photographed me constantly with a vicious little camera he wore around his neck. He sat next to me and wanted to know details of sexual abuse I had suffered. A lovely woman, not knowing that his interest was entirely pornographic, told a terrible story of being molested by a neighbor. He ignored her. She had thought, "This is Allen Ginsberg, the great beat poet and a prince of empathy." Wrong. Ginsberg told me that he had never met an intelligent person who had the ideas I did. I told him he didn't get around enough. He pointed to the friends of my godson and said they were old enough to fuck. They were twelve and thirteen. He said that all sex was good, including forced sex.

I am good at getting rid of men, strictly in the above-board sense. I couldn't get rid of Allen. Finally I had had it. Referring back to the Supreme Court's decision banning child pornography he said, "The right wants to put me in jail." I said, "Yes, they're very sentimental; I'd kill you." The next day he'd point at me in crowded rooms and screech, "She wants to put me in jail." I'd say, "No, Allen, you still don't get it. The right wants to put you in jail. I want you dead."

He told everyone his fucked-up version of the story ("You want to put me in jail") for years. When he died he stopped.

The Bomb

There is one reason for the 1960s generation, virtually all of its attitudes and behaviors: the bomb. From kindergarten through the twelfth grade, every U.S. child born in 1946 or the decade or so after had to hide from the nuclear bomb. None of us knew life without Hiroshima and Nagasaki. In K–3 we hid under our school desks, elbows covering our ears. From grades four or five through graduation, we were lined up three- or four- or five-thick against walls without windows, elbows over our ears. We were supposed to believe that these poses would save us from the bomb the Soviets were going to drop on us sometime after the warning bell rang. In the later grades, our teachers herded us, then stood around and talked. They didn't seem to think that they were going to die, let alone melt, any minute. They seemed more as if they were going to chat until the bell rang and the next class began. In the earlier grades the teachers would walk up and down the aisles and tell us an elbow was outside the boundary of a desk or we should stop giggling. Any child too big to get under the desk wholly and fully might wish the Soviets would nuke us; after all, who wanted to be in school, in rotten school with rotten teachers and rotten classmates? By the time I was being herded in the seventh or eighth grade, I simply refused to go. Not one teacher could explain the logic of elbows over ears in the face of a nuclear onslaught. Not one teacher could explain why they themselves had not flung their bodies up against a wall or why their ears were bare naked and their elbows calmly down by their sides. More to the point as far as I was concerned, not one teacher could explain why, if these were our last few minutes, we should spend them in such an idiotic way. "I'd rather take a walk," I would say, "if I'm about to die now." My father was called in, a scene he described to me shortly before he died at eighty-five: "I asked them what the hell they expected me to do." The real question was, What was one to do with these grown-ups, these liars, these thieves of time and life – my teachers, not the Soviets? Did they expect us to be so dim and dull?

They were helped by the saturation propaganda about both the Soviets and the bomb. *On the Beach* was a really scary novel by Nevil Shute about the last survivors down in Australia. I remember just computing that it wasn't going to be me and maintaining an attitude of anger and disgust at the adults. There were endless television discussions and debates about whether or not one should build a bomb shelter and fill it with canned food and water. The moral question was whether or not one should let the neighbors in, had they been obtuse enough not to build a shelter. Everything was calculated to make one afraid enough to conform. I can remember times wanting my father to build a bomb shelter for the family. Of course that's hard to do in the cement of the city, and by the time we had soil in the suburbs I had decided it was all a scam. Maybe all the students except me and a few others rested wearily against walls and kept quiet, but most of us knew we were being lied to, being scared on purpose, and being treated like chumps, just stupid children. Those boys who didn't know ended up in Vietnam.

I'd read in newspapers and magazines about the people in cities like New York who would not take shelter when the alarms were sounded. Following on the model of the London blitz, sirens would scream and everyone was expected to find hiding in an underground shelter. But some people refused, and they were arrested. I remember writing to Judith Malina of the Living Theatre when she was in the Women's House of Detention in New York City for refusing to take shelter and I was a junior in high school. The thrilling thing was that she wrote me back. This letter back from her was absolute proof that there was a different world and in it were different people than the ones around me. Her letter was a lot of different colors, and she drew some of the nouns so that her sentences were delightful and filled with imagination. Since I had already made myself into a resister, she affirmed for me that resistance was real outside the bounds of my tiny real world. Her letter was mailed from a boat. She was crossing the ocean to

Europe. She wouldn't stay in the United States, where she was expected to hide underground from a nuke. She was part of what she called "the beautiful anarchist nonviolent revolution," and I was going to be part of it, too. I'd follow her to the Women's House of Detention, though my protest was against the Vietnam War, and then to Europe, because I could not stay in the United States any more than she could. She probably didn't have my relatives, who were so ashamed that I went to jail; and she probably didn't have my mother, who said I needed to be caged up like an animal – bad politics twice over. I would not meet Judith for another fifteen years, but she remained an icon to me, the opposite of the loathsome Miss Fox, and I knew whose side I was on, where my bread was buttered, and which one I would rather be. I did not care what it cost: I liked the beautiful anarchist nonviolent revolution, and so did most of my generation – even if "anarchist" was a hard word and "nonviolent" was an even harder discipline.

There was another kind of bomb scare. Someone would phone the school and claim to have hidden a bomb in it. The students would be evacuated and, when the teachers got tired of keeping us in lines, left to roam on the grass. There never was a bomb, and there was no context of terrorism, and the threats seemed only to come in nice weather – otherwise we might all have gotten cranky. We discussed whether or not the grass under our feet felt pain, which teachers had infatuations with each other, how we were going to thrive on poetry and revolution. These were the good bomb scares, after which we'd be remilitarized into study halls and classes and time would pass slowly and then more slowly. There was never anything good about the nuclear-bomb scares, and even the conformists with elbows over ears did not like them. I was appalled that the United States had used nuclear weapons and was now both stockpiling and testing them. My father said that he would have died if not for Hiroshima and Nagasaki, because he shortly would have been sent to "the war in the Pacific" as it was called. When Truman used the nuclear bombs, he saved my father's life. I thought my father was pretty selfish to hold his own life to be more important than so many other lives. I thought it would be a good idea not to have war anymore. I could feel nuclear winter chilling my bones, even though the expression did not yet exist, and I had a vivid picture of people melting. I've never gotten over it.

Cuba 1

There was one day when all my schoolmates and I knew that we were going to die. According to historians the Cuban missile crisis lasted thirteen days, but to us it was one day because we knew we were going to die then, that day. I don't know which of the thirteen it was, and I don't know if I'm collapsing several days into one, but I remember nothing before the one day and nothing after. In the back of the school bus all the girls gathered in a semicircle. We talked about the sadness of dying virgins, though some of us weren't. We spoke with deep regret, like old people looking back on our lives; we enumerated all that we had not managed to do, the wishes we had, the dreams that were unfulfilled. No one talked about getting married. Children came up in passing.

The Soviets had deployed nuclear missiles in Cuba. The missiles were pointed at the United States, and the range of the ICBMs was about from Cuba to the school bus – the northeast corridor of the United States. For probably the first time, I kept my Che-loving politics to myself. I don't think I even had any politics on that day. I don't remember the geopolitical blah-blah or the commie-versus-good-guy rhetoric – except that it existed – or how the United States was the white hat standing up for the purity of the Americas. I do remember television, black-and-white, and the images of still photographs, a grainy black-and-white, showing the bombs or the silos. The United States had been untouchable, and now it could be touched, and we'd feel our own bones melt and in the particle of a second see our own cities drowned in fire. I wasn't afraid to die, but sitting still and waiting for it was not good. I still feel that way. We all, including me, felt a little sorry for ourselves, because everything we had ever known had been touched by nuclear war; it was the shadow on every street, in every house, in every dinnertime conversation, in every current-events reprise; it was always there as threat, and now it was going to happen, that day, then, there, to us. The school bus was bright yellow with black markings on the outside, just the way they are now, but everything was different because we were kids who knew that we were going to be cremated and killed in the same split second. I could see my arm withered, the flesh coming off in paper-thin layers, while my chest was already ash, and there'd be no blood – it would evaporate before we'd even be dead. Inside the bus the boys were up front, boisterous, filled with bravado. I guess they expected to pull the missiles out of the air one by one, new superheroes. The girls were serious and upset. Even those who didn't like each other talked quietly and respectfully. There was one laugh: a joke about the only girl in the school we were sure was no virgin. She was famous as the school whore, and she was widely envied though shunned on a normal day, since she knew the big secret; but on this day, the last day, she could have been crowned queen, sovereign of the girls. She represented everything we wanted: she knew how to do it and how it felt; she knew a lot of boys; she was really pretty and laughed a lot, even though the other girls would not talk to her. She had beautifully curly brown hair and an hourglass figure, but thin. She was Eve's true descendant, the symbol of what it meant to bite the apple. Tomorrow she would go back to being the local slut, but on the day we were all going to die she was Cinderella an hour before midnight. I wished that I could grow up, but I could not entirely remember why. I waited with my schoolmates to die.

David Smith

He was one of the United States' greatest sculptors, not paid attention to now but in my high school and college years he was a giant of an artist. He was especially attached to Bennington College, where he had taught and near where he lived. One night I went to a lecture by art critic Clement Greenberg, probably the most famous visual arts writer of his time. Greenberg was a name-dropping guy, and most of his lecture was about the habits of his betters, the artists he deigned to crown king or prince. At some point during the lecture, Greenberg said that great sculptors never drew. A huge man stood up, overshadowing the audience, and in a deep bass said, "I do." While Greenberg turned beet red and apologized, the big guy talked about how important drawing was, how sensual it was; he gave specifics about how it felt to draw; he said that drawing taught one how to see and that drawing was part of a continuous process of making art, like breathing when you were asleep was part of life. After the lecture a friend who was a painting student asked if I wanted to go with her to meet David Smith. "I wouldn't want to bother him," I said, not having a clue that the big guy was

David Smith and he was staying that night in Robert Frost's old house, owned by painter Kenneth Noland, rented by the English sculptor Anthony Caro, who was teaching at Bennington. We got into my friend's truck and went. I felt shielded by my painter friend. The visit was her brazen act, not mine.

It was my first year at Bennington, and I did not know the anthropology of the place. Anyone famous who came to Bennington was provided with one or more Bennington girls; my college was the archetypical brothel, which may have been why, the semester before I matriculated, the English seniors recreated the brothel in Joyce's *Ulysses* as a senior project and for the enjoyment of the professors.

So my friend and I got to the old Robert Frost house. It was deep in the Vermont countryside, old, simple, painted white, with hooks from the ceiling on which, I was told, animals had been hung and salted. There were bookshelves, but they were mostly empty, with only a few books about Kenneth Noland, at least in the living room. Mr. Smith was deep in a bottle of 100-proof Stolichnaya and scattered like inanimate dolls were some of my fellow students from Bennington, each in a black sheath, each awaiting the pleasure of her host, Anthony Caro, and his guest, David Smith. As happens with habitually drunk fuckers of women, Smith could not have been more indifferent to the women who were there for him, and he wanted to talk to me. I was trying to leave, embarrassed for my classmates and too shy to talk to Smith. But Smith did not have to be nice to the women acquired for him, so he wasn't. He dismissed my fellow students with a gesture of the hand and told me and my friend to sit down and drink with him. He said that he had always wanted to provide Bennington with a graduate school in art; that his name had been on a pro-Cuba petition signed by artists and intellectuals; that John Kennedy had called him up and told him to get his name off of that petition or he'd never get his graduate school; that he had removed his name and in so doing he had whored. "Never whore," he said; "it ruins your art." He told me never to tell anyone and until now, with some private exceptions, I haven't. He's been dead a long time, and that puts him beyond the shame he felt that night. He said that taking his signature off the pro-Cuba petition had made him a whore and he couldn't work anymore because of it. "Work" was literal – it meant making sculptures; "whore" was a metaphor – it meant not compromising one's art. He warned me repeatedly; I only wish he had meant it literally as well as metaphorically because I might have listened. Since then – since I was eighteen – I've always measured my writing against his admonition: never whore. He also taught me how to drink 100-proof Stoli, my drink of choice until in the late 1970s I switched to bottled water and the occasional glass of champagne. He was talking to me, not to my painter friend; I've never known why. I always hoped it was because he saw an artist in me. A week and a half later he died, crashing his motorcycle into a tree, the kind of death police regard as suicide.

Contraception

At some point when I was in junior high or high school, my father gave me the inevitable books on intercourse, more commonly called "how babies are made." He was embarrassed; I rejected the books; he shoved them at me and left the room. I read the books about the sperm and the egg. There were a few missing moments, including how the sperm got to the egg before it was inside the vaginal tract, for example, intercourse, and how not to become pregnant. By the time I was sixteen, I understood the former but not the latter. When I asked my mother, she said that one must never let a man use a rubber because it decreased his pleasure and the purpose was to give him pleasure. Always ready to beat a dead horse into the ground, I elicited from my unwilling mother the fact that she had never let my father use a condom and that she had used birth control. Beyond this she would not go, no hints as to how or what.

One night I was summarily sent to the local Jewish Community Center by my parents acting in tandem. There was to be a lecture on sex education, and I was going to be forced to listen to it. I cried and begged and screamed. I couldn't stand being treated as a child, and I couldn't stand the thought of being bored to death by adults tiptoeing through the tulips. I had learned that adults never told one the real stuff on any subject no matter what it was. It stood to reason that the sex education lecture was going to be stupid and dull, and so it was. There was the sperm and the egg and they met on a blackboard.

By that time I had learned always to listen to what was not being said, to the empty space, as it were, to the verbal void. The key to all adult pedagogy was not in what they did say but in what they would not say. They would say the word "contraception," but they would not say what it was. This was a time in the United States when contraception and abortion were both still illegal. I knew about abortion, or enough about it to suit me then. I asked about contraception and got an awkward runaround. I fucking wanted to know what it was, and they fucking were not going to tell me. I couldn't let it go, as usual, and so got from them the statement that they discussed contraception only with married people. The group that sponsored the lecture, with its almost-famous woman speaker, would not come clean; now that group, headed by the same woman until she died in the last decade, is part of the free speech lobby in the United States protecting the rights of pornographers.

What I learned was simple and eventually evolved into my own pedagogy: listen to what adults refuse to say; find the answers they won't give; note the manipulative ways they have of using authority to cut the child or student or teenager off at the knees; notice their immoral, sneaky reliance on peer pressure to shut up a questioner (because, of course, if one persists, the others in the audience get mad or embarrassed). The writing is in the configuration of white around print; the verbal answer is buried in silence, a purposeful and wicked silence, a lying, cheating silence. Every pregnant girl owes her pregnancy not to the heroic lover who figured out how the sperm gets inside her but to the adults who will not show her a diaphragm, an IUD, a female condom, and – sorry, Ma – a rubber. I left the lecture that night with the certain knowledge that I did not know what contraception was even if I knew the word and that adults were not going to tell me.

Miss Bell, my physical education teacher who also taught health, had the only method that successfully resisted both my Socratic urgency and emerging Kabalistic axioms: on one test paper she mimeographed a huge drawing of the male genitals, and the students had to write on the drawing the name of each part – "scrotum," for instance. In an equivalent test on female sexuality, she had this true-or-false statement for extra credit of twenty points: if a girl is not a virgin when she gets married, she will go to hell. I was the only student in my class not to get the extra twenty points.

Young Americans for Freedom

I wanted to know what a conservative was. I read William Buckley's right-wing magazine *National Review*, as I still do. I knew about the KKK, and I had an idea of what white supremacy was. One girl in my class had neighbors who celebrated Hitler's birthday, which she seemed to find reasonable. I had an English teacher in honors English who was the equivalent of Miss Bell, the gym-health teacher; but because he was more literate there were many paths to hell, not just sex outside of marriage. Told to stay after school one day, I faced Mr. Sullivan as he opposed my reading Voltaire's *Candide*, which was proscribed for Catholics, which I wasn't but he was. He told me I would go to hell for reading it. I stood up to him. I thought he was narrow-minded, but conservatism seemed something different, Buckley's magazine notwithstanding. What was it exactly, and why didn't history teachers or political science types or civics teachers talk about it?

It was a mess just to try to think about it. Walking home from high school one day, I passed a neighbor, Mr. Kane. No one on the street talked to him or his wife, an auburn-haired model. They painted their ranch house lavender, which was downright unusual, though it framed Mrs. Kane's auburn hair beautifully. Mr. Kane called out to me and asked me to come inside the side door to his house. I knew that I was never supposed to talk with strange men or go anywhere with them, and Mr. Kane was strange as hell. But I couldn't resist, because curiosity is such a strong force in a child, or in me. Inside Mr. Kane had literature: he wasn't the sexual child molester, no, he was the political child molester, with endless pamphlets on how JFK, a candidate for president, was the Catholic Church's running dog, so to speak; on how whites were better than what he called niggers; on how kikes were running the media and the country. He gave me leaflets to take home: these went easy on the kikes but hit the Catholics hard. At home I felt ashamed to have even touched the things, and also I knew that I had broken a big law, not a small one, by going with a strange man. I tried to flush the leaflets down our toilet and when they wouldn't flush I tried to burn them. Well, yes, I did get that in the wrong order but I was guilty of fairly heinous crimes and was desperate to get rid of the evidence. I was just trying to find a shovel to dig a hole in the backyard where I could bury them when my mother came home. She saw the stuff, dripping wet all over, an additional sin I hadn't thought of, and sent me to my bedroom to wait for my father. I knew the stuff was filthy and bad, my own behavior a mere footnote to the sinister material I had brought into the house. It's amazing how seeing hate stuff and touching it can make one viscerally sick.

I was called out into the living room. My mother and father were sitting on the formal sofa that we had and I was expected to stand. My father had the junk beside him on the sofa. He had called the FBI. They were going to come and question me. They came and they did. Mr. Kane disappeared from the street and Mrs. Kane would stand out on the lawn, her auburn hair crowning her beauty, alone; she was now alone. Their house was eventually sold.

The crime, it turned out, was to threaten a candidate for president of the United States. The dirty drawings and words were taken to be direct threats against Kennedy, as were the vile insults targeted to the Catholic Church and the pope. I, too, was punished, but not by the government. I can't remember what the punishment was, but it was tempered with mercy because I had helped shut down a hate enterprise. I knew that Mr. Kane was not a conservative in the way that Mr. Buckley was, even though Mr. Buckley supported segregation, to my shock and dismay.

To find out what was and was not conservative as such, I approached a group called Young Americans for Freedom. Their leader was a somewhat aristocratic man named Fulton Lewis III. This was far outside any prior experience of mine. I wanted to debate him. I set up the debate for a school assembly. I hurled liberal platitude after liberal platitude at him. He won the debate. This made me question not my beliefs in equality and fairness but how one could communicate those beliefs. I felt the humiliation of defeat, of course. I don't like losing, and I was stunned that I did lose. Still, the home team had lost because students thought that Mr. Lewis III was correct. These were the years of the John Birch Society and *None Dare Call It Treason*, a book in which commies and socialists were hidden in every nook and cranny of the government and the media, and the point was that these equality-minded folks were Soviet dupes, low and venal. I didn't see how my classmates could think being against poverty or for integration were Soviet ideas or treasonous ideas. Mr. Lewis was exceptionally gracious.

This was the beginning for me of thinking about something the entertainer Steve Allen, a liberal, had written in *National Review*. Roughly paraphrased, Mr. Allen's piece asked why a person was categorized as just a liberal or just a conservative. Wasn't that same person also a musician or a teacher and a husband and a father? The patrilineal approach was the only approach in those days, liberal or conservative. I thought it was probably wrong to hate people for their politics unless they were doing evil, as Mr. Kane was. The argument remains alive; the stereotypes persist, veiled now in a postcommie rhetoric; I think that hate crimes are real crimes against groups of people, imputing to those people a lesser humanity. And even though I've lost debates since the one with Mr. Lewis III, I still think it's worth everything to say what you believe. There are always consequences, and one must be prepared to face them. In this context there is no free speech and there never will be.

I think especially of watching William Buckley, on his *Firing Line* television program in the 1960s, debate the writer James Baldwin on segregation. Buckley was elegant and brilliant and *wrong*; Baldwin was passionate and brilliant and wore his heart on his sleeve – he was also right. But Buckley won the debate; Baldwin lost it. I'll never forget how much I learned from the confrontation: be Baldwin, not Buckley.

Cuba 2

The bad news came first from Allen Young, a gay activist: in Cuba homosexuals were being locked up; homosexuality was a crime against the state. A generation later I read the work of Reinaldo Arenas, a homosexual writer who refused to be crushed by the state and wrote a florid, uncompromising prose. I read the prison memoirs of Armando Valladares and heard from some friends raised in Cuba and original supporters of Castro and Che about whole varieties of oppression and brutality. There was also more recently a stunning biography of Che by John Lee Anderson that gave Che his due – cold-blooded killer and immensely brave warrior. Of course, the river of blood and suffering makes it hard to say why so many of us, from David Smith to myself, saw so much hope in the Cuban revolution. Batista's thuggery was indisputable; his thievery, too, from a population of the exceptionally poor and largely illiterate was ugly; but the worst part of it was U.S. support for his regime. That support made many of us challenge the political morality of the United States. Castro claimed he wanted an end to poverty and illiteracy, and I believed him. Castro up against Batista is the mise-en-scène. With Castro the poor would have food and books. Castro also promised to stop prostitution, which had destroyed the lives of thousands of poor women and children; prostitution was considered one of the perks of capitalism, and Havana in particular was known for prostitution writ large. Where there was hunger, there would be women and children selling sex. Now we would know to look for other phenomena as well: incest or child sexual abuse, homelessness, predatory traffickers. It would have been hard to think of Castro as worse than Batista outside the context of the cold war. When the tiny band of guerrilla fighters conquered Havana and extirpated the Batista regime, it was hard to mourn unless the prospect of equality, which was the promise, inevitably meant tyranny (which I think is the right-wing argument). Virtually forced by the United States into an alliance with the Soviets, Castro's system of oppression slowly supplanted Batista's. Watching the United States now cuddle with the Chinese because Chinese despotism is rhetorically committed to capitalism, one can only mourn the chance lost to the Cuban people thirty-some years ago when the United States might have been a strategic ally or neighbor. I'm saying that the United States pushed Cuba into the Soviet camp and that Castro became what he became because of it.

The Grand Jury

I was eighteen; it was 1965; a grand jury had been impaneled to investigate the charges I had made against New York City's Women's House of Detention, the local Bastille that sat in the heart of Greenwich Village, in the heart of Bohemia itself. I had been sexually brutalized and had turned the internal examinations of women in that place into a political issue that would eventually topple the ancien régime, the callous, encrustated Democrats.

I had been subpoenaed to testify on a certain day at a certain time. My French class at Bennington was also on that day, at that time, and I was hopeless in the language. My French professor took my haplessness in French rather personally and refused to give me permission to miss the class. I explained that I had to be absent anyway, and I was. She backed off of her threat to give me a failing mark and gave me a near-failing mark instead.

I stayed at a friend's apartment in New York the night before my testifying, and Frank Hogan, New York City's much-admired district attorney, came with another man that night to see *me*. The magnitude of his visit is probably not self-evident: the big pooh-bah, prosecutor of all prosecutors, came to see me. He seemed to want to hear from me that I would show up. I assured him that I would. Just be yourself and tell the truth, said the snake to Eve. I assured him that I would. He kept trying to find out if I was wary of testifying or of him. I wasn't. I was too stupid to be. The rules have since changed, but in 1965 no one, including the target of a grand jury investigation, could have a lawyer with her inside the sacred, secret grand jury room. I was not the target, but one would not have been able to tell from what the assistant district attorney did to me. Hogan had assured me that all the questions would be about the jail and pretty much said outright that the jail had to go, something to that effect. He probably said sympathetically that he had heard it was a horrible place and I assumed the rest. After all, if it was horrible, why wouldn't one want to get rid of it? The grand jury room was big and shiny wood and imperial. I sat down in what increasingly came to seem like a sinking hole and had to each side and in front of me raised desks behind which were washed white people, most or all men. The assistant district attorney, who had been with Mr. Hogan the night before but had said nothing, began to ask me questions. Where did I live? Did I live alone? Was I a virgin? Did I smoke marijuana? I started out just being confused. I remembered clearly that Mr. Hogan said the inquiry was about the jail, not me, so I answered each question with some fact about the jail. Did I live alone? They knew I was living with two men. I described the dirt in the jail or the excrement that passed for food. Did I smoke marijuana? Was I going to betray the revolution by saying no? On the other hand, was I going to give the grand jury an excuse to hold for the righteousness of the jail by saying yes? I answered with more details about the jail. And so it went for several hours. I eventually got the hang of it. The pig would ask me a personal question, and I would answer about the jail. He got angrier and angrier, and I stayed soft-spoken but firm. They could have jailed me for contempt, but they didn't want me back in jail. I had created a maelstrom for them; because of the news coverage, which was, for its time, massive, huge numbers of people in the United States and eventually around the world knew my name, my face, and what had been done to me in the jail. Putting me back in jail could only make the situation for Mayor Robert Wagner, head of the corrupt city Dems, more difficult. I had spoken on the same platform as John Lindsay, a liberal Republican who would eventually become mayor, and I had something to do with making that unlikely event happen. After I testified I went back to college. While probation would have been the normal status for someone not yet convicted of anything and released on her own recognizance, I was on parole, which allowed me to cross state lines to go back to school without violating the court's rules. The system was being so good to me.

A couple of months later there was an article in the *New York Times* saying that the grand jury had found nothing wrong with the jail. Everything had hinged on my testimony, so they were also saying that I was a liar. I left the country soon after, but seven years later, when the place was finally closed, a lot of people thanked me. Years later Judith Malina would say I had done it. When I challenged that rendering of the politics, she said that political generation after political generation had tried but I had succeeded – not that I had done it alone, of course not, but that without what I had done, for all anyone knew the jail would still be there, thirteen floors of brutalized women. Most of the women in the Women's House of Detention when I was there and in the immediate years before and after were prostituted women; I had the unearned dignity of having been arrested for a political offense. Frank Hogan had a street named after him after he died.

Probably the best moment for me happened one day when I was approached by a black woman on a Village street corner while I was waiting for a light. She worked in the jail, she said, and couldn't be seen talking with me, but she wanted me to know that everything I had said was true and she was one of many guards who was glad I had managed to speak out. You tell the truth and people can shit all over it, the way that grand jury did, but somehow once it's said it can't be unsaid; it stays living, somewhere, in someone's heart.

The Orient Express

I was going to Greece. There were two countries in Europe where one could live cheaply – Greece and Spain. The fascist Franco was still in power in Spain, so I decided on Greece. I took a boat, the appropriately named *SS Castel Félicé*, from New York to a port in the south of England, then a train to London. I had two relatives there, old women, hard-core Stalinists, who talked energetically and endlessly about the brilliant and gorgeous subway stations in Leningrad. It's a disorienting experience – listening to the worship of a subway system. They saw me off on that legendary train the Orient Express. It has since been rehabilitated, but in 1965 it was a wretched thing. I had under $100 and the clothes I wore along with some extra underwear and T-shirts. We changed trains in Paris in some dark, damp, underground station, and we kept going south. Somewhere outside of Paris people began exiting and cattle began coming on. There was no food, no potable water; as the train covered the terrain downhill we'd get more cows accompanied by a peasant or a peasant family. I hadn't anticipated this at all – I, too, had read about the elegant and mysterious Orient Express. A sweet boy offered to share his canned Spam with me, but I foolishly declined. It was a four-day trip from London to Athens, each hour after Paris more sordid than the one before. I did love the train ride through Yugoslavia because the country was so very beautiful, and I promised myself I would go back there someday, a bad promise nullified by war. I had never been in a communist country; there were more police than I had ever seen in my life, and each one wanted to see everyone's passport and go through everyone's luggage. I was easy on that score. I had one small piece of luggage and nothing more.

While still in Yugoslavia, I began talking with an American named Mildred. She was wrinkled as if her skin had been white bread, squooshed and rolled and then left to dry. She had smudges of lipstick here and there and was very kind to me. I needed water desperately by the time we reached Yugoslavia, but I was afraid to run out to the station when the train stopped because I didn't know when it would start up again. I've always found traveling by train exhausting and anxiety-making. Mildred gave me water or pop or something I could drink. The cows were in touching distance now, and so were the peasants, though there were many more cows than peasants.

Mildred was going to Athens. Someone had stolen all of her money. She wondered if she could borrow some from me – what I had would be exactly enough for her to liberate her things, being held by an irate landlord, and then later that same day she would have the money wired to her by her son so she would be able to pay me back. We made a date to meet in a town square in Athens for the day following our arrival. I gave Mildred pretty much all of my money. I had enough for the YWCA that first night. The next day at the appointed hour I waited in the square. She never came. The direct consequence was that as it started turning dark I had to find a man to take me to dinner and get me a room. And I would have to do the same the next day and the day after that. I kept hoping I'd find Mildred here or there. I never held it against her.

Easter

I went to Crete to live and write. I didn't know much about it except that my roommate at the Y was from there. What I found was heaven on earth: the bluest sky; water in bands of turquoise, lavender, aqua, and silver; rocks so old they had whole histories written on the underside of their rough edges; opium poppies a foot high and blood red; a primitive harbor; caves in which people lived; peasants who came down from the mountains to the city for political speeches – there would be a whole family in a wooden cart pulled by a mule with an old man walking the mule; there was light the color of bright yellow and bright white melted together, and it never went away; even at night, somehow through the dark, the light would manifest, an unmistakable presence, and in the darkest part of night you could see the tiniest pebble resting by your foot. This was an island on which old women in black cooked on Bunsen burners, olive trees were wealth, and there was a universal politics of noli me tangere with a lineage from 400 years of Turkish occupation through Nazi occupation; the people were fierce and proud and sometimes terribly sad.

The place changed for me one day. It was Easter. I was with an English friend and a Greek lover. The streets began filling up with gangs of men carrying lit torches. They seemed a little KKK-ish. Their intentions did not seem friendly. My Greek lover explained that the gangs were looking for Jews, the killers of Christ. That would be me. My companions and I hid behind a pillar of a church. I don't think there were other Jews on the island, because this search for Christ's killers had gone on year after year, even before the Turkish occupation. I wondered if the gang of men would kill me. I thought they would. I was afraid, but the worst of it was that I was afraid my Greek lover would give me up – here she is, the Jew. I was the faithless one, because this question was in my heart and mind. I wondered what would happen if the torches found us, saw us and took us. I wondered if he'd stand up for me then. I wondered how the people I'd been living with could turn into a malignant crowd, a hate crowd. If there were no other Jews on the island, it was because they had been killed or had fled. (Tourist season had not yet begun.)

The next day teenaged boys dove into the Aegean Sea to look for a jeweled cross blessed by the Orthodox priest and thrown by him into the water; one boy found it and emerged like an elegant whale from the water, cross raised above his head as high as he could hold it. The sun and the cross merged into an astonishing brightness, the natural and the man-made making the boy into some kind of religious prince. It was beautiful and savage, and I could see myself bleeding out the day before, a corpse on cold stone.

Knossos

I didn't know anything about anthropology or the reconstruction of the ancient Cretan palace of Knossos by the English archeologist Sir Arthur Evans. I didn't know it was the labyrinth of Daedalus or the palace of King Minos, the Minotaur symbolizing generations of sacralized bulls. I had no idea of the claims that would be made for it later by feminists: the bull was the sacred animal of Goddess religions and cults, the symbol of the Great Goddess. One of the great icons of modern feminism originates in Crete – the labyris, the double ax. Both the bull and the labyris signified the Goddess religion, and Knossos was a holy site. From 3,700 years before Christ to 2,000 years before Christ, Crete was the zenith of civilization, a Goddess-worshiping civilization.

Originally I saw it from the opposite side of the road. A friend and I went to have a picnic in the country north of Heraklion; we had wine and a Greek soft cheese that I particularly favored; we were in love and trouble and so talked in our own pidgin tongue made up of Greek, English, and French. I found myself going out there alone and finding refuge in the intriguing building across the road, Knossos. I found the throne room especially lovely and intimate. I would take a book, sit on the throne, and read, every now and then thinking about what it must have been like to live in this small and intimate room. The rest of the palace that had been restored was closed, and as soon as I heard the first busload of tourists sometime in late April I never went back. But for a while it was mine. I felt at home there, something I rarely feel anywhere. Once I was inside, it was as familiar as my own skin. I loved the stone from which everything, including the throne, was made. I loved the shape of the room and the throne itself. I loved the colors, as I remember them now mostly red and blue but very pure, the true colors painted on stone. I don't think it is possible to go back to a place that has such a grip on one's heart; or I can't. When I die, though, I'm going back, as ash, dust unto dust – not to the stone walls or throne of Knossos but to a high hill overlooking Heraklion. I belong to the place even if the place does not belong to me.

Kazantzakis

In the early morning I would walk from my balcony near the water to the market. I'd buy olives. There had to be dozens of different kinds. Of all the food for sale, olives were the cheapest, and I'd buy the cheapest of those – about an eighth of an ounce – and then I'd find a café and order a coffee. I'd keep filling the cup with milk, each time changing the ratio of coffee to milk. I'd have the waiter bring more and more milk. As long as there was still some coffee in the cup I couldn't be refused. This was a rule I made up in my mind, but it seemed to hold true. Early on I stole a salt shaker so that I could clean my teeth. Salt is abrasive, but it works.

I had read about the square where I took my coffee in Nikos Kazantzakis's novel *Freedom or Death*, a book I carried with me almost everywhere once I discovered it (and I still have that paperback copy, brown and brittle). A novelist who captures the soul of a country or a people writes fiction and history and mythology, and *Freedom or Death* is such a work. It is the story of the 1889 revolt of the Cretans against the Turks. It is epic and at the same time it is the story of Heraklion, Crete's largest city and where I was living. Inside the epic there are love stories, stories of fraternal affection and conflict, sickening details of war and occupation. In the square – the square where I was sitting – the Turks would hang rebels, the solitary body often more terrifying than any baker's dozen. Only a writer can show that precise thing, bring the disfigured humanity of the dead individual into one's own viscera. One forgets the eloquence of the single person who wanted freedom and got death. I could always see the body hanging.

In those days political women did a kind of inner translating so that all the heroes, almost always men except for the occasional valiant female prostitute, were persons, ungendered, and one could aspire to be such a person. The point for the writer and other readers might well be masculinity itself, but the political female read in a different pitch – the body shaking the trees with its weight, obstructing both wind and light, would be more lyrical, with the timbre in Billie Holiday's voice. *Freedom or Death* set the terms for fighting oppression; later, feminism brought those terms to a new maturity with the idea that one had to be willing to die for freedom, yes, but also willing to live for it. Each day over my prolonged cup of coffee I would watch the body hanging in the square and think about it, why the body was displayed in torment as if the torture, the killing continued after death. I would feel the fear it created in those who saw it. I would feel the necessity of another incursion against the oppressor – to show that he had not won, nor had he created a paralyzing fear, nor had he stopped one from risking one's life for freedom.

I haven't read Kazantzakis since I lived on Crete in 1965. I have never read *Zorba the Greek*, his most famous novel because of the movie made from the book, a movie I saw maybe a decade or two later on television. Freedom or death was how I felt about segregation back home, the Vietnam War, stopping the bomb, writing, making love, going where I wanted when I wanted. Freedom or death was how I felt about the Nazis, the fascists, the tyrants, the sadists, the cold killers. Freedom or death was how I felt about the world created by the compromisers, the mediocrities, the apathetic. Freedom or death encapsulated my philosophy. So I wrote a series of poems called *(Vietnam) Variations*; poems and prose poems I collected in a book printed on Crete called *Child*; a novel in a style resembling magical realism called *Notes on Burning Boyfriend*; and poems and dialogues I later handprinted using movable type in a book called *Morning Hair*. The burning boyfriend was Norman Morrison, the pacifist who had set himself on fire to protest the Vietnam War.

Discipline

I learned how to write on Crete. I learned to write every day. I learned to work on a typewriter that I had rented in Heraklion. I had thin, light blue paper. I'd carve out hours for myself, the same every day, and no matter what was going on in the rest of my writer's life I used those hours for writing. I learned to throw away what was no good. One asks, How does a writer write? And one asks, How does a writer live? At first one imitates. I imitated in those years Lorca, Genet, Baldwin, D. H. Lawrence, Henry Miller. I read both Miller and Lawrence Durrell on being a writer in Greece. It seemed from them as if words could stream down with the light. I did not find that to be the case, and so I thought that perhaps I was not a writer. Then one wants to know about the one great book: can someone young write only one book and have it be great – or was there only one Rimbaud for all eternity and the gift is all used up? Then one needs to know if what one wrote yesterday and the day before has the aura of greatness so that the whole thing, eventually, would be the one great book even though that might have to be followed by a second great book. Then one wants to know if the greatness shows in one's face or manner or being so that people would draw back a little on confronting the bearer of the greatness. Then one wants to know if being a writer is like being Sisyphus or perhaps Prometheus. One wants to know if writers are a little band of gods created in each generation, cursed or blessed with the task of finding themselves – finding that they are writers. One wants to know if one will write something important enough to die for; or if fascists will kill one for what one writes; or if one can write prose or poetry so strong that nothing can break its back. One wonders if one will be able to stand up to or against dictators or police power. One wonders if one has the illusion of a vocation or if one has the vocation. One wonders about how to be what one wants to be – that genius of a writer who takes literature to a new level or that genius of a writer who brings humanity forward or that genius of a writer who tells a simple, gorgeous story or that genius of a writer who holds hands with Dostoyevsky or Tolstoy or that genius of a writer who lets the mute speak, especially the last, letting the mute speak. Can one make a sound that the deaf can hear? Can one write a narrative visually accessible to the blind? Can one write for the dispossessed, the marginalized, the tortured? Is there a kind of genius that can make a story as real as a tree or an idea as inevitable as taking the next breath? Is there a genius who can create morning out of words and can one be that genius? The questions are hubristic, but they go to the core of the writing project: how to be a god who can create a world in which people actually live – some of the people being characters, some of the people being readers.

The Freighter

I learned how to listen from my father and from being on the freighter. My father could listen to anyone: sit quietly, follow what they had to say even if he abhorred it – for instance, the racism in some of my family members – and later use it for teaching, for pedagogy. Through watching him – his calm, his stillness, the sometimes deep disapproval buried under the weight of his cheeks, his mouth in a slight but barely perceptible frown – I saw the posture of one strong enough to hear without being overcome with anger or desperation or fear. I saw a vital man with a conscience pick his fights, and they were always policy fights, in his school as a teacher, as a guidance counselor, in the post office where he worked unloading trucks. For instance, in the post office where he was relatively powerless, he'd work on Christian holidays so that his fellow laborers could have those days with their families. I saw someone with principles who had no need to call attention to himself.

The ocean isn't really very different, though it can be more flamboyant. It simply is; it doesn't require one's attention; there is no arrogance however fierce it can become. I took a freighter from Heraklion to Savannah to New York City. In the two and a half weeks on the ocean, I mainly listened: to the narrative of Tolstoy's *War and Peace*, which I read some of every day; to the earth buried miles under the ocean; to the astonishing stillness of the water, potentially so wild and deadly, on most nights blanketed by an impenetrable darkness; to the things living under and around me; to the crew and captain of the ship; to the one family also making the trek, the sullenness of the teen, the creativity of a younger child, the brightness of the adults' optimism.

It seems a false analogy – my father and the ocean – because my father was a humble man and the ocean is overwhelming until one sees that it simply is what it is. From my father and from the ocean, I learned to listen with concentration and poise to the women who would talk to me years later: the women who had been raped and prostituted; the women who had been battered; the women who had been incested as children. I think that sometimes they spoke to me because they had an intuition that the difficulty in saying the words would not be in vain; and in this sense my father and the ocean gave me the one great tool of my life – an ability to listen so closely that I could find meaning in the sounds of suffering and pain, anger and hate, sorrow and grief. I could listen to a barely executed whisper and I could listen to the shrill rant. I knew never to shut down inside; I learned to defer my own reactions and to consider listening an honor and a holy act. I learned patience, too, from my father and from that ocean that never ends but goes round again circling the earth with no meaning, nothing outside itself. One need not go to the moon to see the cascading roundness of our globe because the ocean shows it and says it; there are a million little sounds, tiny noises, the same as in a human heart. Had I never been on the freighter I think I would never have learned anything except the tangled ways of humans fighting – ego or war. The words on Kazantzakis's grave say, "I hope for nothing, I fear nothing, I am free." On the freighter and from my father I learned the final lesson of Crete, and it would stand me in good stead years later in fighting for the rights of women, especially sexually abused women: I hope for nothing; I fear nothing; I am free.

Strategy

After I lived on Crete, I went back to Bennington for two long, highly psychedelic years. There I fought for on-campus contraception – a no-no when colleges and universities functioned in loco parentis – and legal abortion. I fought against the Vietnam War. I tried to open up an antiwar counseling center to keep the rural-poor men in the towns around the college from signing up to be soldiers. Most of these were white men, and Vietnam was the equivalent of welfare for them. But the burning issue was boys in rooms. Bennington, an all-girls' school with a few male students in dance and drama, had parietal hours: from 2 a.m. to 6 a.m. the houses in which the students lived were girls only. One could have sex with another girl, and many of us did, myself certainly included. But the male lovers had to disappear: be driven out like beasts into the cold mountain night, hide behind trees during the hour of the wolf, and reemerge after dawn. The elimination of parietal hours was a huge issue, in some ways as big as the war. In colleges across the country girls were required to be in their gender-segregated dormitories by 10. Girls who went to Bennington in the main valued personal freedom; at least this girl did. As one watched male faculty sneak in and out of student bedrooms, one could think about lies, lies, lies. As one saw the pregnancies that led to illegal abortions from these liaisons, one could think about the secret but not subtle cruelty of fully adult men to young women. Everyone knew the Bennington guard who was deaf, and one prayed he would be on the 2-to-6 shift so one could have sex with a man one's own age without facing suspension or expulsion. When a student would go with a boy to a motel, she could expect a call at the motel from a particular administrator, a lesbian in hiding who tried to defend law and order. It was law and order versus personal freedom, and I was on the side of personal freedom.

The college had a new president, Edward J. Bloustein, a constitutional lawyer, or so he said. The U.S. Constitution is amazingly malleable. Regardless, he was a law-and-order guy, and he didn't belong at Bennington. You might say it was him or me. He wanted a more conventional Bennington with a more conventional student body and a fully conventional liberal-arts curriculum. He wanted to expand the student body, which would make classes bigger. He wanted all the hippies gone and all the druggies gone and all the lesbian lovers gone. He was for abstinence at a time when virginity before marriage was highly prized; he was against abortion and once told me in a confrontation we had in his office that Jewish girls tried to get pregnant – thus the problem with pregnancy on campus. That was a new one. He considered the faculty blameless.

Feeling under siege by this gray, gray man, students elected me to the Judicial Committee of the college. It was clear that he was looking for a scapegoat, someone to expel for defying parietal hours especially but also for smoking dope and having girl-girl sex. The students knew I could stand up to him, and I could. The scapegoat he wanted to punish was my best friend, and he just fucking was not going to get the chance to do it.

She had been seen kissing another girl on the steps inside the house in which she lived. I've rarely met a Bennington woman from that time who does not think that she herself was the girl being kissed. Someone reported my friend for shooting up heroin in the living room. I recently asked her if she had, and she said no. In the thirty-five years that I've known her, I've never known her to lie – which was the problem back then. The college president confronted her on marijuana use, and she told him the truth – that she only had a joint or two on her right then. Knowing her, I'd bet she offered to share.

The house where I lived, Franklin House, was a hotbed of treason, so first we had her move there. She could not quite grasp the notion of turning down music while people were sleeping, and in our house that was a crime. One could shoot up heroin or kiss girls, but one could not be a nuisance. Nevertheless, everyone knew a lot was at stake and so the music blared. To protect the personal freedom of each person living in Franklin we seceded from the school. We declared ourselves entirely independent and we voted down parietal hours. So stringy, hairy boys were in the bathrooms at 4 a.m., as one of the few female professors noted in outrage at one of the many public meetings. If they weren't bothering anyone, it was no crime. If they were, it could be bright and sunny and mid-afternoon and it was a crime. We elected an empress, an oracle, and other high officials. (I was the oracle, though I preferred the title "seer.") This was a pleasant anarchy. No one had to live there who didn't want to, but my best friend was not going to be homeless because some rat ass was upset by some deep kissing.

The secession heightened the conflict between students and the administration. It was just another version of adults lying, having a pretense of order, as the foxes on the faculty sneaked into the henhouse with impunity. They impregnated with impunity. They paid for criminal abortions with impunity.

The apocalypse was coming. Each day the class warfare between students on the one side and faculty and administration on the other intensified. The lying, cheating faculty began to piss a lot of us off. They always presented themselves as being on our side against the administration because this was how they got laid, but slowly the truth emerged – they wanted the appearance of professorship during the day and randy access to the students at night, between 2 and 6 being hours that carried a lot of traffic. As the tension grew, my best friend was closer and closer to being tied down on the altar and split in half.

I worked out a plan. The school was governed by a constitution. The Judicial Committee had the right to expel students. My plan was to call a school meeting, ask everyone to submit a signed piece of paper saying that she had broken the parietal hours, and then expel everyone, as we had the right to do. Out of a student body of a few hundred students, only about six refused. The Judicial Committee expelled everyone else. In effect the school ceased to exist.

It's always the law-and-order guys who turn to tyranny when they've been legally beat. In this case Bloustein exercised raw power. He waited until graduation before reacting; he sent a letter to all the expelled students' parents that said they could not come back to school unless they signed a loyalty oath to obey the school's rules. I didn't go back to school. I would never sign any such oath. But I thought his tactic was disgusting: it's bad to break the spirit of the young, and that's what he did. In order to go back to school, students had to betray themselves and each other, and most did. I learned never to ignore the reality of power pure and simple. I also learned that one could get a bunch of people to do something brave or new or rebellious, but if it didn't come from their deepest hearts they could not maintain the honor of their commitment. I learned that one does not overwhelm people by persuading them to do something basically antagonistic to their own sense of self; nor can rhetoric create in people a sustained determination to win. I thought Bloustein did something evil by making students sign that oath; how dare he? But he dared, they did, and I left sickened.

Suffer the Little Children

In Amsterdam I knew a hippie man whose children from an early marriage were coming to stay with him. They were thirteen and eleven, I think. The older girl had been incested by her stepfather. This came into the open because the older girl tried to kill herself. This she did at least in part valiantly because she saw the stepfather beginning to make moves on the younger girl in exactly the same way he had gradually forced himself on her. The stepfather had started to wash and shower with the younger girl. The mother, in despair, wrote the hippie man, who had abandoned all of them, for help. She wanted to mend the relationship with the second husband while keeping her children safe. The hippie man made clear to those of us who knew him that he considered his older daughter responsible for the sex; you know how girls flirt and all that. His woman friend made clear to him that he was wrong and also that she was not going to take care of the children. She wouldn't have to, he said; he would be the nurturer. When the girls arrived in Amsterdam, one recently raped, the other exceptionally nervous and upset by temperament or contagion or molestation, the hippie man forgot his vows of responsibility, as he had always forgotten all the vows he had ever made, and let all the work, emotional and physical, devolve on his woman friend. She wasn't having any and simply refused to take care of them. Eventually she left.

One night I got a call from her: the hippie man had given each kid 100 guilders, set them loose, and told them to take care of themselves. He just could not be with them without fucking them, he told her (and them). In a noble and compassionate alternative gesture, he put them out on the streets. His woman friend made clear to me that this was a mess she was not going to clean up. I asked where they were.

They had taken shelter in the frame of an abandoned building, squatters without a room that had walls. They lived up toward the wooden frame for the ceiling. Their light came from burning candles. I found them and took them home with me, although "home" would be stretching it a bit. At that moment I lived in an emptied apartment, the one I had lived in with my husband, a batterer. I had married him after I left Bennington for the second time (the first was Crete, the second Amsterdam). After I had played hide-and-seek with the brute for a number of months, he decided I could live in the apartment he had cleaned out. By then I was grateful even if it meant that he knew where I was. A woman's life is full of such trade-offs. So when the girls came with me, it wasn't to safety or luxury or even just enough. The apartment, however, did have walls, and one does learn to be grateful.

The older girl thought that she was probably pregnant. Her father, the hippie man, did light shows, many for rock bands; he had the habit of sending musicians into the older girl's bed to have sex with her; the younger daughter slept next to the older girl, both on a mattress on the floor. They were wonderful and delightful girls, scared to death; each put up the best front she could: I'm not afraid, I don't care, none of it hurts me.

The first order of business, after getting them down from the wood rafters illuminated by the burning candles, was getting the older one a pregnancy test. If she was pregnant, she was going to have an abortion, I said. I'm not proud now of using my authority that way, but she was a child, a real child; anyway, for better or worse, I would have forced one on her. In Amsterdam the procedure was not so clandestine nor so stigmatized. It turned out that she wasn't pregnant.

One day she was suddenly very happy. One of the adult rockers sent into her bed by her father was going to Spain and he wanted to take her. This was proof that he loved her. I knew from the hippie father that he had paid the rocker to take the girl. Finally I was the adult and someone else was the child. I told her. I told her carefully and slowly and with love but I told her the truth, all of it, about the rotten father and the rotten rocker. Her mother now wanted her and her sister back. I sent them back. Nothing would ever be simple for me again. A strain of melancholy entered my life; it was the fusion of responsibility with loss in a world of bruised and bullied strangers.

Theory

I went to Amsterdam to interview the Provos – not the blood-soaked Irish Provos but the hashish-soaked Dutch ones. They served as the prototype for the U.S. yippies, though their theory was more sophisticated; as one said to me, "Make an action that puts crowds of ordinary people in direct conflict with the police, then disappear. This will undermine police authority and politicize those they beat up." The man I eventually married said that he envisaged social change as circles on a canvas; the idea was to destabilize the circles by adding ones that didn't fit – the canvas would inevitably lose its integrity and some circles would fall off, a paradigm for social chaos that would topple social hierarchies.

What I found infinitely more valuable, however, were three books: *Sexual Politics* by Kate Millett; *The Dialectic of Sex* by Shulamith Firestone; and *Sisterhood Is Powerful*, an anthology edited by Robin Morgan. These were the classic, basic texts of radical feminism; what happened when women moved to the left of the left. I was hardheaded though; I defended Norman Mailer even though his attacks on Millett were philistine; I still liked D. H. Lawrence, though now I find him unbearable to read, such a prissy and intolerant hee-haw; and I again learned the power of listening, this time because of someone who listened to me.

Her name was Dr. Frankel-Teitz. I had found out that when you told people your husband was beating you, they turned their backs on you. Mostly they blamed you. They said it wouldn't be happening if you didn't want it and like it. You could be, as I was, carrying all you could hold in an effort to escape or you could be, as I was, badly hurt and bleeding, and they still told you that you wanted it. You could be running away fast and furious, but it was still your will, not his, that controlled the scenario of violence: you liked it. You could ask for help and they'd deny you help and it was still your fault and you liked it. I'd like to wipe out every person on earth who ever said that to or about an abused woman.

I had a lot of physical problems from having been beaten so much and from the tough months of running and hiding, including terrible open sores on my breasts from where he burned me with a cigarette. The sores would open up without warning like stigmata and my breasts would bleed. Finally women helping me found me a doctor. "All the lesbians go to her," they said, and in those days that was a damned good recommendation. I went to her but was determined not to say I had been beaten or I was running; I couldn't bear one more time of being told it was my fault. Still, I said it; it fell out of me when she saw the open sores. "That's horrible," she said –

about the beatings, not the sores. I'll never forget it. "That's horrible." Was she on my side; did she believe me; was it horrible? "No one's ever said that," I told her. No one had.

A few years later, back in the United States, I sent Dr. Frankel-Teitz a copy of *Woman Hating* and a letter thanking her for her help and kindness. She replied with a fairly cranky letter saying that she didn't see what the big deal was; she had only said and done the obvious. The obvious had included getting me medicine I couldn't afford. I thought that she was the most remarkable person I had ever met. "That's horrible." Can saving someone really be that simple? "That's horrible." Horrible, that's horrible. What does it take? What's so hard about it? How can the women who don't say those words live with themselves? How can the women who do say those words now, thirty years later, worry more about how they dress and which parties they go to? In between the early days and now someone must have meant what she said enough so that it could not be erased. How much can it cost? Horrible, that's horrible.

The Vow

It was a tender conversation. The woman who had helped me most in Amsterdam, Ricki Abrams, sat with me and we held hands. I was going to go back to New York. I talked with Ricki about how she had saved my life; I thanked her. I talked with Ricki about having prostituted and having been homeless. Back then I never talked about these parts of my own life. I talked with her about bringing what I had learned into the fight for women's freedom. I talked with her about my fierce commitment to the women's movement and feminism. I talked to her about how grateful I was to the women's movement – to the women who had been organizing and talking and shouting and writing, making women both visible and loved by each other. I talked with her about the book she and I had started together and that I was going to finish alone, *Woman Hating*. We had shown a draft of the chapter on *Suck*, a counterculture pornography magazine, to those who ran the magazine, ex-pats like ourselves, from the same generation, with the same commitment to civil rights and, we thought, human dignity. They cut us cold. Ricki could not stand it. I could. There's one thing about surviving prostitution – it takes a hell of a lot to scare you. My husband was a hell of a lot, and he taught me real fear; the idiots at *Suck* were not much of anything. Writing had become more important to me than the irritability of wannabe pimps.

Sitting with Ricki, talking with Ricki, I made a vow to her: that I would use everything I knew, including from prostitution, to make the women's movement stronger and better; that I'd give my life to the movement and for the movement. I promised to be honor-bound to the well-being of women, to do anything necessary for that well-being. I promised to live and to die if need be for women. I made that vow some thirty years ago, and I have not betrayed it yet.

I took two laundry bags filled with manuscripts, books, and some clothes, the Afghan sheepskin coat I had as a legacy from my marriage, an airplane ticket given me by a junkie, and some money I had stolen, and I went back to New York City. Living hand to mouth, sleeping on floors or in closet-sized rooms, I began working on *Woman Hating*. I had up to four jobs at a time. Every other day I would take $7 out of a checking account. I ate at happy hours in bars. Any money I had I would first tithe to the Black Panther Party in Oakland, California. Huey Newton sent me his poems before he shot and killed a teenage prostitute, the event that caused him to flee the United States. Since I didn't believe that the police had framed him, one might say that a rift had opened between him and me. But I still kept sending money for the breakfast and literacy programs sponsored by the Black Panthers.

I went to demonstrations as often as I could. The Three Marias of Portugal had written a feminist book that got them jailed. I demonstrated in their behalf. I went to prolesbian and antiapartheid demonstrations.

One of my part-time jobs was organizing against the Vietnam War, the backdrop to most of my life as a young adult. In Amsterdam my husband and I had helped deserters from the U.S. military hide on their way to Sweden. Vietnam had been shaping my life since I was eighteen and was sent to the Women's House of Detention. The poet Muriel Rukeyser, who also worked against the war, hired me as her assistant. Muriel had a long and distinguished life of rebellion, including the birth of a son out of wedlock in an age darker than any I had experienced. He was now a draft resister in Canada. With another woman, Garland Harris, I organized a conference that brought together artists and intellectuals against the war. Robert Lifton, Susan Sontag, and Daniel Ellsberg participated. With director André Gregory I helped organize a special night on which all the theaters and theater companies in Manhattan would donate their money to help rebuild a hospital in North Vietnam that U.S. bombs had leveled. I was not really able to face the chasm between the left and feminism even though I gloried in the essays in *Sisterhood Is Powerful* that exposed the sexism of the left. I couldn't stop working against the war or, for instance, apartheid just because the men on the left were pigs. I became part of a consciousness-raising group, but even that had its roots in the Speaking Bitterness sessions in communist China. I worked hard. One of my mentors, the writer Grace Paley, who had helped me when I got out of the Women's House of Detention, helped me again – this time to get an apartment. It was on the Lower East Side, in an old tenement building. The toilet was in the hall and the bathtub was in the kitchen. I had a desk, a chair, and a $12 foam-rubber mattress. I bought one fork, one spoon, one knife, one plate, one bowl. I was determined to learn to live without men.

My Last Leftist Meeting

There were only seven of us. I was the menial, a part-time office worker. The movie director Emile D'Antonio seemed to lead the meeting by sheer force of personality. There were three women, including myself. That translated into six eminents, two of whom were women. Our goal was to find the next project for celebrities organized against the war in a group called Redress. The idea of the group was 100 percent Amerikan: famous people organized to fight the war, their names having more pull than those of professional politicians or ordinary citizens. It was a time when fame was not disso-ciated from accomplishment: most of our members had earned through achievement whatever fame they had. But the hierarchy of fame always favored those in the movies; intellec-tuals per se were low on the list. As an office worker, I was not expected to have ideas, but I had them anyway. In the larger meetings when we had a whole roomful of the famous or somewhat famous, I would be cut in two for putting an idea forward. I remember being torn to pieces by some famous divinity professor. Whoever he is, I hate him now as much as I did then. Another noneminent and I apparently called his moral purity into question. I have no idea how or why; I didn't then and I don't now.

In this smaller meeting in a tiny room around a nondescript table there was more congeniality. Cora Weiss was there, I remember – her family owns or owned Revlon. A man named Carl from Vietnam Veterans Against the War headed the meeting in the official sense; he was famous in the antiwar movement, prominent, in no way a servant, instead a rather cunning leader. The women's movement was going full tilt but never seemed to penetrate the antiwar movement (and hasn't, in my opinion, to this day). No one appeared willing to rethink the status quo. In fact, no one was prepared to understand that the women's movement had outclassed the peace movement with both its originality and its vision of equality.

I had once been at a meeting at Carl's apartment, shared with a woman. He proudly showed me the self-hating graffiti her consciousness-raising group had etched and drawn and painted onto a canvas on the wall. He enjoyed it a lot and especially, as he made clear to me, that the women had done it themselves. See, he seemed to be saying, this is what they think of themselves so I don't have to think more of them. I remember being very troubled – why was this woman-hating graffiti what they thought of themselves? I remember noting in my mind that this was part of the problem, not part of the solution.

We took a break in the middle of our little meeting – some-one had to make a phone call – but returned to the table well before the break was over. None of the women, including myself, talked. Our colleagues of the male persuasion did talk: about Marilyn Chambers, the pornography star who had sold Ivory soap in television commercials until she was booted out by a morals clause in her Ivory contract. The conversation came from out of nowhere; nothing logically led to it and nothing explained the fact that the men all liked the conversa-tion and participated happily. They talked in particular about how much they would like to fuck her in the ass. This seemed to derive from her most famous movie, *Behind the Green Door*, which they all seemed to have seen.

I sat there in dismay and confusion. Weren't we trying to stop exploitation? Weren't we the love children, not the hate children? Didn't we believe in the dignity of all persons? Wasn't it clear – surely it didn't have to be pointed out – that pornography defamed women? Even if Carl's woman friend and her friends debased themselves, commercial pornography required male consumption and brought the defamation to a new level. What the men said was so vile that I was really wounded by it. I seemed unable to learn the lesson that porno-graphy trumped political principle and honor. (I may have learned it by now.)

I found myself nauseated and in my mind debated whether or not I would give a little exit speech or simply get up and leave. The exit speech would have the advantage of letting them know how they had let down me and mine, others like me, women. Were these men worth it – were they worth fighting for the right words, which was always so hard? Were they worth overcoming the nausea, or should I just puke on the table (and I was damned close to it)? I noted that the men were having a good time and that the women not only did not raise their eyes but had their heads lowered as if trying to pretend they didn't hear or weren't there. I noticed that the men did not notice that the women had suddenly become absent, at the table yes but not present, not verbal – there was a quiet resembling social or political death; in effect, the women were erased. I got up and walked out. I never went back to the group and stopped getting my $75-a-week paycheck, which was the mainstay of my existence. Everything else I earned was chump change.

Petra Kelly

Some twenty years after my last leftist meeting, I went to a memorial service at the United Nations Chapel for Petra Kelly.

Petra Kelly was the daughter of an Amerikan father and a German mother; she was a pacifist and a feminist. Living in Germany she founded the Green Party, which was devoted to ecofeminism, nonviolence, and antipornography politics. She brought one of the first lawsuits against a pornographer for slander, libel, and hate. She put up a hell of a fight but lost the case. The lefties within the Green Party didn't support her. Before her death she was doing antiwar work in the Balkans.

The memorial service was organized and attended by my old pacifist friends from the anti–Vietnam War days. Petra had been shot to death by her male companion-lover who then shot and killed himself. The companion-lover had been a general with NATO in Germany; Petra had been responsible for his transformation into a pacifist.

Cora Weiss was the emcee of the event. There were seven or eight invited speakers, most of them male or maybe all of them but Bella Abzug. Many of the speakers, touched by the conversion of the NATO general to nonviolence, spoke at length about his courage and honor, his stunning contributions to pacifism and world peace (through renouncing NATO). Some of them mentioned Petra in passing. One or two did not mention her at all but called him "brother" and nearly dissolved in tears. (And we thought that boys couldn't cry.) The sentimentality on behalf of the male convert to pacifism was astonishing. Many of the speakers appeared to accept that Petra and her companion-lover were the victims of a plot, probably CIA, because the CIA saw him as a turncoat and wanted to kill him – she was, as monsters say, collateral damage. Others thought that there had been a mutual suicide pact, that Petra had agreed – ladies first – to be killed by the former NATO general. I waited for Bella Abzug, one of my heroes, to speak. She spoke last, I think, but nothing she said challenged the notion of Petra as a helpmate who wanted to be killed. She even managed to say something nice about the boy, though she nearly choked on the words. I was devastated.

I got up to go to the front to speak. I was not on the agenda. Cora motioned me back to my seat and said in a loud whisper that there wasn't time for anyone else to say anything. She gestured in a way that implied she couldn't be more sorry. I forced myself through the ropes that marked the speaking area and kept it sacrosanct. I turned to face the audience of mourners. Here were men I had known since I was eighteen – from my earliest days in fighting against the war in Vietnam. I couldn't believe that nothing had changed – peace, peace,

peace, love, love, love; they did not understand nor would they even consider that a man had murdered a woman.

I said that while Petra's life had been extraordinary her death was not; it was an ordinary death for a woman. Petra had been killed by her lover, her intimate, her mate. She was killed in her bed wearing a nightgown. (I knew but didn't say that Petra would never commit suicide by any means while unclothed or even partly exposed – the pornography of it would have been repellent to her. She also would never have used a gun or allowed its use.) She had probably been asleep. Nothing could be more commonplace or cowardly. The audience of pacifists started hissing and some started shouting. I said that there was probably no conspiracy and certainly no acquiescence on the part of Petra; everything in her life and politics argued against any such complicity. It had to be faced, I said, that pacifists had not taken a stand against violence against women; it was still invisible to them, even when the woman was Petra Kelly, a world-class activist. I said that the male's life meant more to them than hers did. By this time the pacifists were in various stages of rage.

No pacifist woman stood up to support me, though Petra would have. I said that, hard as it was, one had to understand that Petra had died like millions of other women around the world: prematurely, violently, and at the hands of someone who was presumed to love her. I said that nonviolence was not possible if the ordinary, violent deaths of women went unremarked, unnoticed. However extraordinary Petra had been in her life, I repeated, her death could not have been more commonplace.

The mourners were angry. Some were shouting nasty names at me. I said that I had to speak because not to do so would be to betray Petra's work and the work we had done together, in concert. I ran from the room. One woman grabbed my arm on my way out. "Thank you," she said. That's enough; it has to be enough – one on-site person during a conflict showing respect.

I felt that I had stood up for Petra. I knew she would have stood up for me.

Capitalist Pig

I started speaking and lecturing as a feminist because I had a lot of trouble getting my work published. I spoke on violence against women. In the early years of the women's movement, this subject was marginal, violence itself considered an anomaly, not intrinsic to the low status of women. I accepted that valuation; I just thought that this was work I could do and therefore had to do. When something's got your name on it, you're the one responsible for finding a way to create an awareness, a stand, a set of strategies. It's yours to do. There can be 100,000 others with their names on it, too, but that doesn't get you off the hook.

I spoke in small rooms filled with women, and afterward someone would pass a hat. I remember a crowd of about fifty in Woodstock, New York, that chipped in about $60. I slept on the floor of whoever had asked me or organized the event, and I ate whatever I was given – bad tabbouleh stands out in my mind. I needed money to live on but didn't believe in asking for it from women, because women were poor. Women's centers in towns and on college campuses were poor. Sometimes a woman would pass me a note that had a check in it for $25 or some such sum; the highest I remember was $150, and that was a fortune in my eyes.

I had to travel to wherever the speech was in the hope that I'd be able to collect enough money to pay for my expenses. Flo Kennedy often talked about how if you did not demand money people would treat you badly. I did not believe that could be true, but for the most part it was. I can remember the gut-wrenching decision to ask for a fee up front, first $200, then $500. A few years later I got a speaking agent, Phyllis Langer, who had been an editor at Ms. She took a 25 percent commission, whereas most speaking or lecture agents took a full 33 percent. By the time I hired her, I was making in the $1,500–$3,000 range. She made sure that I got paid, that the event was handled okay, with publicity, and that expenses were reimbursed. She was kind and also provided perspective. When she went to work at an agency that I didn't particularly like, I decided to represent myself. By this time my nervousness about money had disappeared, a Darwinian adaptation, although my stage fright – which has run me ragged over the years – never did.

I would call whoever wanted me to speak on the phone. I'd get an idea of how much money they could raise. I still wanted them to be comfortable, and it was a horror to me that anyone would think I was ripping them off. By the time I took over making all the arrangements myself, I had developed a fixed set of necessities: a good hotel room in a good hotel, enough money for meals and ground transportation (taxis, not buses or subways). Eventually I graduated to the best hotel I could find, and I'd also buy myself a first-class ticket.

Representing myself, I would fold an estimate of expenses into a fee so that the sponsor had to pay me only one amount, after I spoke on the night that I spoke. I had developed an aversion to having organizers vet my expenses, even though I was scrupulous. If I watched an in-room movie, I paid for it myself.

In the first years, I was so poor that if I spoke at a conference I usually could not afford a ticket for the inevitable concert scheduled as part of the conference. I didn't know that I could get one for free. If I wanted a T-shirt from the conference, I couldn't buy it. My favorite women's movement button – "Don't Suck. Bite" – cost too much for me to have one. I was scraping by, and the skin was pretty torn from my fingers.

Even during the early years, I got letters from women telling me that I was a capitalist pig; yeah, they did begrudge me the $60. It wasn't personal. It was just that any money I earned came from someone else who also didn't have enough money for a T-shirt. Or did she? I guess I'll never know. I couldn't embrace being a capitalist pig; I couldn't accept the fact – and it was a fact – that the more money I was paid, the nicer people were. I couldn't even accept the good fallout – that charging a fee for a lecture enabled me to do benefits as well. After a while I got the hang of it and when work fell off, when the speaking events dried up, when someone was nasty to me, I just raised my price. It was bad for the karma but good for this life.

I remember that saying I was poor got me contempt, not empathy or a few more dollars. I remember that begging for money especially brought out the cruelty in people. I remember that trying to talk about poverty – you show me yours and I'll show you mine – never brought forth anything other than insult. Competitive poverty was the lowest negotiation, a fight to the moral death.

In hindsight it is clear to me that I never would have been able to put in more than a quarter of a century on the road had I not figured out what I needed. Everyone doesn't need what I need, but I do need what I need. Money is a hard discipline, not easy to learn, especially for the lumpen like me.

One Woman

I was walking down the street on a bright, sunny day in New York City sometime in 1975. A woman almost as bright and sunny was walking toward me. I recognized her, an acquaintance in the world of books. She had been up at my Woodstock speech, which had been about rape. I had started writing out my speeches because of my frustration at not being able to find venues for publication. This was called "The Rape Atrocity and the Boy Next Door," subsequently published in 1976 in a collection of speeches called *Our Blood: Prophecies and Discourses on Sexual Politics*. We greeted each other, and then she started talking: she had been raped on a particular night in a particular city years before. She had left the window open just a little for the breeze. The guy climbed in and when she awoke he had already restrained her wrists and was inside her. We stood in that one place for an hour or so because she told me every detail of the rape. Most of them I still remember.

I gave the same speech at a small community college. At the reception after, the host pulled me aside. She had been gang-raped some fifteen years before. The rapists were just about to be released from prison. She was in terror. One key element in their convictions was that they had taken photographs of the rape. The prosecutor was able to use the photographs to show the jury the brutal fact of the rape.

Some eight years later a founder of one of the early rape crisis centers told me that she and her colleagues were seeing increasing numbers of rapes that were photographed; the photography was part of the rape. The photographs themselves no longer proved that a rape had taken place. For the rapists, they intensified pleasure during the rape and after it they were tokens, happy reminders; but the perception of what the photograph meant had changed. No matter how violent the rape, the photograph of it seemed to be proof of the victim's complicity to increasing numbers of jurors.

Everywhere that I traveled, starting from my poorest days in New York and its environs to my more lucrative days flying around the country to my sometimes-rich – sometimes-poor days on the international level, I had women talking to me about having been raped; then about having been raped and photographed. One simply cannot imagine the pain. Each woman told the story in the same way: no detail was left out; the clock was running and the whole story had to be told to me, then, there, wherever we were. Six months or a year or several years could have passed since they had come to hear me speak; six months or fifteen years could have passed since the rape or the rape and the photographs.

Women did not stand up after the speech and speak about

a personal experience of rape; the questions were socially acceptable and usually abstract. It was when they saw me somewhere, anywhere really, but alone, that they told me, sometimes in whispers, what had happened to them. I had to live with what I was being told.

Like death, rape happens to one woman, an individual, a singular person. Even in circumstances of war when there is mass rape, each rape happens to one woman. That one woman can be raped many times by one man or by many. I've spent the larger part of my adult life listening to stories of rape. At first I listened naïvely, surprised that a woman walking down the street on a bright and sunny day, someone I really did not know, could, after a greeting, launch into a sickening, detailed story of a rape that had happened to her. The element of surprise never entirely went away, but later I would be certain to steel myself, balance my body, try to calm my mind. I couldn't move, I could barely breathe – I was afraid of hurting her, the one woman, by a gesture that seemed dismissive or by a look on my face that might be mistaken for incredulity.

Most of the rapes were unreported; some were inside families; each rape was in some sense a secret; one woman and then one woman and then one woman did not think she would be believed. The political ground in society as a whole was not welcoming. The genius of the New York Radical Feminists was that they organized a speak-out on rape in the early 1970s before anyone was prepared to listen. They paved the way.

The genius of Susan Brownmiller's book *Against Our Will: Men, Women and Rape* was that it gave rape a history. The genius of the women's movement was in demanding that rape be addressed as a social policy issue. A consequence of that demand was legal reform, some but not enough. The rules of evidence shamelessly favor the accused rapist(s) and destroy the dignity of the rape victim. The rape victim is still suspect – this is a prejudice against women as deep as any antiblack prejudice. She lied, she lied, she lied: women lie. The bite marks on her back show that she liked rough sex, not that a sexual predator had chewed up her back. That she went with her school chum to Central Park and her death – she was strangled with her bra – proved that she liked rough sex. One woman was tortured and raped by her husband; he was so arrogant that he videotaped a half hour, including his use of a knife on her breasts. The jury, which had eight women on it, acquitted – they thought that he needed help. He. Needed. Help.

In the old days – or, to use the beautiful black expression, "back in the day" – it was presumed that the woman was sexually provocative or was trying to destroy the man with a phony charge of rape. Now in the United States the question is repeated ad nauseam: is she credible? For this question to have any meaning, one would have to believe that rapists pick their victims based on the victims' credibility. "Oh, she's credible; I'll rape her." Or, "No, she's not credible; I'll wait until a credible one comes by."

The raped woman still stands accused in the media, especially if she has named the rapist. For one woman to say "I was raped" is easier than for one woman, Juanita Broderick, to say "I was raped by William Jefferson Clinton." Ms. Broderick told us that she was raped and by whom; no one has held him accountable in any way that matters.

It Takes a Village

It happens so often that I, at least, cannot keep track of it. A woman is only believed if and when other women come forward to say the man or men raped them, too. The oddness of this should be transparent: if I'm robbed and my neighbor isn't, I'm still robbed – there is no legal or social agreement that in order for me, the victim of a robbery, to be believed, the burglar has to have robbed my neighbors. As writer Chris Matthews said, "There are banks that Willy Sutton didn't rob."

I remember an early, terrible case in which a woman with a history of mental upheaval due to her father's incestuous rape of her was raped by her psychiatrist. She had no credibility, as they say, and the jury was doing a full-tilt boogie toward vindicating the accused.

No one noticed a famous character actor who came to the trial every day. The actor sat quietly and used her formidable skill to help herself disappear. As the case was heading to the jury, which was going to acquit, the actor came forward: exactly the same thing had happened to her – father-daughter incest and rape by this same psychiatrist. The actor testified and the media printed pictures of her. Because of the actor's familiarity to a large audience and the obvious terror she felt in exposing herself, the jury did not find for the rapist. How do I know that the terror was real? I talked with her.

In that case what no one seemed to understand was why the victim, raped twice now by persons who were supposed to protect and care for her, raped twice now by figures of power and authority, was unstable – of course she was. Since she had no credibility precisely because of the effects of the two rapes on her, she needed rescue by the actor. Once the actor testified, there were other women prepared to testify, and it was because of the other women waiting in the wings that the defense collapsed. In fact, the psychiatrist knew by virtue of his learning and expertise that incested women were staggeringly vulnerable and easy to shame; he bet his reputation and professional life that shame would shut them up no matter how egregious his sexual abuse of them.

It takes a village of women to nail a rapist. Some rapists of children have molested or assaulted hundreds of children before they are caught for their first offense. Rapists of adult women are high-brow and low-brow, white trash and black trash, cunning and brutal, smart and stupid; some are high achievers; some are rich; some are famous. Since the woman is always on trial – this time to be evaluated on her credibility – there almost always needs to be more than one of her to attest to the abuser's predatory patterns.

This was one of the great roles that rape crisis centers played:

patterns would emerge; women who could not bring themselves to go to the law could provide a lot of data on active rapists; even without appearing in court, the knowledge that there were other victims might give a prosecutor some balls in bringing a case and trying to get a conviction for the one woman, by definition not credible enough. In the early days, it was still thought that women could not argue court cases, so there were virtually no female prosecutors.

Each time the women's movement achieves success in providing a way for a woman to speak out, in court or in the media, the prorape constituency lobbies against her: against her credibility. It's as if we're going to have a vote on it, the new reality TV: are we for her or against her? Is she a liar or – let's be kind – merely disturbed? In the United States it is increasingly common to have the lawyers defending the accused rapist on television talk shows. The victim is slimed; the jury pool is contaminated; what happens to the woman after the trial is lost; she's gone, disappeared, as if her larynx had been ripped out of her throat and even her shadow had been rent.

The credibility issue is gender specific: it's amazing how with all the rapes there are so few rapists. If one follows the misogynistic reporting on rape, one has to conclude that maybe there are five guys. The worst thing about a legal system that puts the worth of the accused above the worth of the victim is that the creep almost always looks clean: somebody's father, somebody's brother, somebody's son. Don't you care? we used to ask; she's somebody's daughter, somebody's sister. The answer was unequivocal: no, we don't give a fuck. Worse was the saccharine sweetness of those who pretended to care about somebody's mother, somebody's sister. I've heard at least a dozen criminal defense lawyers say, "I have a sister; I have a daughter; I have a wife." The rapists they defend use the same locution. They want us to believe that the problem is that this one woman wasn't raped and the accused didn't do it. Even though criminal defense lawyers will admit that they rarely have innocent clients, each time the public takes the sucker punch: I have a sister; he has a sister; see his pretty suit; look at how well groomed he is. Her, she's a mess. Well, yes, she's been raped; it kind of messes you up. Oh, now we're playing victim, are we? Advice to young women: try not to be his first, because then there aren't others to confirm your story. You can't earn credibility; you can't buy it; you can't fake it; and you're a fucking fool if you think you have any.

Hillary Rodham Clinton's husband is so good at sliming the women he's abused – and he has had so much help – that it might take two villages.

True Grit

Becoming a feminist – seeing women through the prism of feminism – meant changing and developing a new stance. For instance, I hate prisons, but the process of becoming a feminist made me face the fact that I thought some people should be in jail. Years later, after watching rapists and batterers go free almost all the time, my pacifism would collapse like a glass tower, leaving me with jagged cuts everywhere inside and out and half-buried as well. I began to believe that the bad guys should be executed – not by the state but by the victim, if she desired, one shot to the head.

When I was still a baby feminist (this being the lingo of the movement), I was asked to go and interview a felon named Tommy Trantino, who had published a book of drawings and stories called *Unlock the Lock*. The person who had asked me to go thought that I could write something about Trantino that might help to get him out.

I went to Rahway State Prison, a maximum-security prison in New Jersey. I talked to Trantino in a small, transparent room, almost all glass. I was surrounded by the prison population, not in lockdown. Trantino had been convicted of killing two cops. I read a lot about him before I went. The same day on which he had killed the cops he had also beaten up a couple of women.

I asked Trantino all the obvious questions, including "Did you do it?" His response was that he didn't remember. Then I departed from the script. I said that I knew he had been in jail a long time, but had he heard of the women's movement and what did he think of it? Hands in his pants pockets, he spread his legs wide open and said, "Well, I'm good with women and I'm bad with women." That was enough for me, but ever the intrepid reporter I said that I had noted that he had beat up two women on the day of the killings; did he think he would still beat up on women if he was out? His answer was an equivocating no, but I heard yes as clear as church bells on a Sunday, and as far as I was concerned he could stay in jail forever. I didn't think that this was the right way to think, but I couldn't stop thinking it.

I began the Socratic course of discussing the problem with my friends, still mostly on the pacifist left. Everyone told me, in different ways, that I had an obligation to help Trantino get out: prison was the larger evil. Here I was, virtually overlooking the murders of the two policemen; but he hit those women, and I didn't think there was anything to suggest that if or when he was out he wouldn't hit more women.

One weekend someone took me to a benefit for one of the pacifist groups. I was so offended by the antiwoman lyrics to a song that I got up and walked out. Someone else did, too. We reached the pavement at approximately the same time. "I have a question I'd like to ask you," I said to the stranger. I then presented the Trantino problem, which was really gnawing at me. "It sounds like you already know what you want to do," he said. Yes, I nodded. "You want him to stay in, right?" "Yes," I said out loud. The man was John Stoltenberg, and I've lived with him for nearly twenty-seven years. I called up the friend who had asked me to write the piece and said I couldn't do it. I told her the true reason: the women, not the police.

Anita

The same friend asked me to go talk with Anita Hoffman, whose husband, Abbie, had just gone underground after being busted for selling cocaine. I had donated some money to Abbie's defense fund and said he should just keep running. I didn't really know why I was going to see Anita.

The apartment was small and crowded, distinguished only by a television set the size of a small country. Anita's child with Abbie, America, was playing. She and I sat on what was her bed to talk.

She and Abbie had not been together for a while. It was clear that she was poor. She said that she didn't know what to do, that a friend of Abbie's had offered her work as a prostitute ("escort," high end of the line) and was putting a lot of pressure on her. Abbie's latest caper had left her destitute. This guy was a friend of Abbie's, so he had to be okay, right? She had thought of doing organizing – poor, single mothers like herself who had no political power in the system; but really, what was wrong with prostituting? She could earn a lot of money and she was lonely. Honey, I thought, you don't begin to know what lonely is.

I told her about my own experiences in the trade, especially about the dissociation that was essential to doing the deed. You had to separate your mind from your body. Your consciousness had to be hovering somewhere near the ceiling behind you or on the far side of the room watching your body. No one got through it without having that happen. I also told her that she'd begin to hate men; at first manipulating them would seem like power, but eventually and inevitably the day would come when one perceived them as coarse and brutal, smelly, dirty bullies. She had said that she liked sex and that she had had sex with the guy who was now trying to pimp her. I told her that the sex with Abbie's friend was a setup to make her more pliant and that in prostituting one lost the ability to feel, so if one liked sex it was the last thing, not the first thing, that one should do. I told her that most people thought that women prostituted in order to get money for drugs, but it was the other way around; the prostitution became so vile, so ugly, so hard, that drugs provided the only soft landing, a kind of embrace – and on the literal level they took away the pain, physical and mental.

I didn't see or talk to Anita again after that night, but the friend who had asked me to go said that Anita had moved to California and had a job as an editor. I don't know if Anita ever tried the prostituting, but if so I helped her get out fast and if not I helped with that, too. I was lucky to have the chance to talk with her, and I began to understand that my own experiences could have meaning for other women in ways that mattered. I began to trust myself more.

Prisons

Perhaps because I came from the pacifist left, I had an intense and abiding hatred for prisons (even though the U.S. prison system was developed by the Quakers). After the publication of *Our Blood*, I wrote a proposal for a book on prisons. I was struck by the way prisons stayed the same through time and place: the confinement of an individual in bad circumstances with a sadistic edge and including all the prison rites of passage. I was struck by how prisons were the only places in which men were threatened with rape in a way analogous to the female experience. I was struck by the common sadomasochistic structure of the prison experience no matter what the crime or country or historical era. That proposal was rejected by a slew of publishers. I found myself at a dead end.

But an odd redemption was at hand. I had noticed that in all pornography one also found the prison as leitmotif, the sexualization of confining and beating women, the ubiquitous rape, the dominance and submission of the social world in which women were literally and metaphorically imprisoned.

I decided to write on pornography because I could make the same points – show the same inequities – as with prisons.

Pornography and prisons were built on cruelty and brutal-ization; the demeaning of the human body as a form of pun-ishment; the worthlessness of the individual human being; restraint, confinement, tying, whipping, branding, torture, penetration, and kicking as commonplace ordeals. Each was a social construction that could be different but was not; each incorporated and exploited isolation, dominance and submis-sion, humiliation, and dehumanization. In each the effort was to control a human being by attacking human dignity. In each the guilt of the imprisoned provided a license to animalize persons, which in turn led to a recognition of the ways in which animals were misused outside the prison, outside the pornography. Arguably (but not always), those in prison had committed an offense; the offense of women in porno-graphy was in being women. In both prisons and pornogra-phy, sadomasochism was a universal dynamic; there was no chance for reciprocity or mutuality or an equality of commu-nication.

In prison populations and in pornography, the most aggressive rapist was at the top of the social structure. In prison populations gender was created by who got fucked; so, too, in pornography. It amazed me that in pornography the prison was recreated repeatedly as the sexual environment most conducive to the rape of women.

The one difference, unbridgeable, intractable, between prisons and pornography was that prisoners were not expected to like being in prison, whereas women were supposed to like each and every abuse suffered in pornography.

Sister, Can You Spare a Dime?

In 1983 Catharine A. MacKinnon and I drafted, and the City of Minneapolis passed, a civil law that held pornographers responsible for the sexual abuse associated with the making and consuming of pornography. If a woman or girl was forced into making pornography or if a woman or girl was raped or assaulted because of pornography, the pornographer or retailer could be held responsible for civil damages. If a woman was forced to view pornography (commonplace in situations of domestic abuse), the person or institution (a school, for instance) that forced her could be held responsible. The burden of proof was on the victim. In addition, the law defined pornography as sex discrimination; this meant that pornography helped to create and maintain the second-class status of women in society – that turning a woman into an object or using her body in violent, sexually explicit ways contributed to the devaluing of women in every part of life. The pornography itself was defined in the statute as a series of concrete scenarios in which women were sexually subordinated to men.

In 1984 I went with a group of activists and organizers to the convention of the National Organization for Women in order to get NOW's support for this new approach to fighting pornography.

The convention was held in New Orleans in a posh hotel. Sonia Johnson, an activist especially associated with a radical crusade to pass the Equal Rights Amendment, was running for president of NOW, and she surrendered her time and space so that I could address the convention on her behalf; our understanding was that I would talk about pornography and the new approach MacKinnon and I had developed.

It was a hot, hot city in every sense. Leaving the hotel one saw the trafficking in women in virtually every venue along Bourbon Street. The whole French Quarter, and Bourbon Street in particular, was crowded with middle-aged men in suits roving as if in gangs, dripping sweat, going from one sex show to the next, searching for prostitutes and strippers.

In the hotel, NOW women were herded into caucuses and divided into cliques. I'm a member of NOW, even though its milksop politics deeply offend me. Now I was going to try to persuade the members that they should pursue the difficult and dangerous task of addressing pornography as a civil rights issue for women.

It is hard to describe how insular NOW is. It is run on the national level by women who want to play politics with the big boys in Washington, D.C., where NOW's national office is located. I had, over the years, spoken at rallies and events organized by many local NOW chapters all over the country. On the local level, my experience with NOW was entirely wonderful. The members were valiant women, often the sole staff for battered women's shelters and rape crisis centers, often the only organized progressive group in a small town or city. I've never met better women or better feminists. Those who run the nationally visible NOW are different in kind: they stick to safe issues and mimic the politics and strategies of professional political lobbyists.

Soon after I came back from Amsterdam, I spoke at a rally organized by the local NOW chapter in Washington, D.C. At the time the burning issue was the Equal Rights Amendment, a proposed amendment to the U.S. Constitution that would have given women a basic right to equality. There was a lot of official (national) NOW literature on the Equal Rights Amendment that I saw for the first time in D.C. I couldn't understand why reading it made me question the ERA – a question I had only on contact with national NOW, its literature and its spokespeople. But of course, I did understand – I just wasn't schooled yet in the ways of this duplicitous feminist organization. The literature was all about how the ERA would benefit men. Guts were sorely lacking even back then.

A decade later, the organization was torn over pornography. The big girls in the big office didn't want to get their hands dirty – the issue demanded at least an imagined descent down the social ladder. Lots of local NOW activists were fully engaged in the fight against pornography and brought those politics to the convention. Then there were what I take to be honorable women who believed the pornographers' propaganda that the civil rights approach would hurt freedom of speech. Then there were the women, a small but determined group, who thought that equality meant women using pornography in the same ways that men did. We wanted a resolution from NOW supporting the civil rights approach. We got it, but, speaking for myself, at great emotional cost.

NOW runs its meetings using Robert's rules of order, which is democracy at its most degraded. One had to know whether to hold up a red poster or a green poster or a yellow poster to be recognized by the chair to speak. I can't even now articulate the points of order involved. When I got home, I dreamt about those posters for months.

A vote was held on whether I could speak for Sonia Johnson. The women voted no. So much for free speech. In place of addressing the whole convention, we organized a meeting to which anyone interested could come. I was speaking, and in the middle NOW cut off the electricity for the mike. More free speech. I was in tears, really. The woman who cut off the juice and then physically repossessed the mike – just following orders, she said – claimed that we had not followed the rules for holding our meeting. We had, but never mind.

Then the most miraculous thing happened. We had a suite

in the hotel, as did other subgroups of NOW, so that people could come by, talk, pick up literature, find out for themselves who we were and what we believed.

I was approached by a black woman who worked in the hotel and asked if we would march down Bourbon Street with the workers in the hotel and the local chapter of the Association of Community Organizations for Reform Now (ACORN) to protest the pornography and prostitution so densely located there. This woman might well have made my bed that morning. It was an overwhelming mandate. Of course we said yes and tried to get the NOW women to join, which they pretty solidly refused to do.

New Orleans is like most other cities in the United States in that the areas in which pornography and prostitution flourish are the areas in which poor people, largely people of color, live. We were being invited to stand up with them against the parasitic exploitation of their lives, against the despoiling of their living environment.

The group was poor. They took packages of paper plates, wrote on the plates "No More Porn," and stuck the inscribed plates up on storefronts and bars all along Bourbon Street. Demonstrators also carried NOW logos. There were maybe a hundred people marching (as opposed to the thousand or so back in the hotel). I was privileged to speak out on the street with my sisters, a bullhorn taking the place of a microphone.

Meanwhile someone in the leadership of NOW had called the police to alert them to an illegal march, a march without a permit. As our rally came to an end and we were marching out of the French Quarter the police approached. We ran. They arrested one of us at the back of the line. He, an organizer from Minneapolis, went to jail for the night, a martyr for the feminist cause. And it became a bad feminist habit for the rich to rat out the poor, turn on the poor, keep themselves divided from the poor – no mixing with the dispossessed. The ladies with the cash to go to New Orleans from other parts of the country did not want to be mistaken for the downtrodden.

The Women

The first time a woman came up to me after a speech to say that she had been in pornography was in Lincoln, Nebraska – at a local NOW meeting in the heartland. I knew a lot about pornography before I started writing *Pornography: Men Possessing Women* because, as an intellectual, I had read a lot of literary pornography and because, as a woman, I had prostituted. In pornography one found the map of male sexual dominance and one also found, as I said in a speech, "the poor, the illiterate, married women with no voice, women forced into prostitution or kept from getting out and women raped, raped once, raped twice, raped more times than they [could] count."

Pornography brought me back to the world of my own kind; I looked at a picture and I saw a live woman.

Some women were prostituted generation after generation and, as one woman, a third-generation prostitute, said, "I've done enough to raise a child and not make her a prostitute and not make her a fourth generation."

I found pride – "I got a scar on my hand; you can't really see it, but a guy tried to slice my throat, and I took the knife from him and I stabbed him back. To this day I don't know if he's dead, but I don't care because he was trying to take my life."

I found women whose whole lives were consumed by pornography: "I've been involved in pornography all my life until 1987. I was gang-raped, that's how I conceived my daughter, and she was born in a brothel in Cleveland, Ohio"; the child "was beaten to death by a trick – she used to get beat up a lot by tricks. I've often wondered if some of the physical damage that was done to her simply [was because] maybe a child's body wasn't meant to be used that way, you know. Maybe babies aren't meant to be anally penetrated by things or snakes or bottles or by men's penises, but I don't know for sure. I'm not really sure about that because that's what my life was."

This same woman has "films of pornography that was taken of me from the time I was a baby until just a few years ago."

I even found women wanting something from the system: "I wish that this system, the courts and, you know, our judicial system that's supposed to be there to help would have done something earlier in our life. I wish they would have done something earlier in our daughter's life and I wish that they would do something now."

Women in pornography and prostitution talked to me, and I became responsible for what I heard. I listened; I wrote; I learned. I do not know why so many women trusted me enough to speak to me, but underneath anything I write one can hear the percussive sound of their heartbeats. If one has to pick one kind of pedagogy over all others, I pick listening. It breaks down prejudices and stereotypes; it widens self-imposed limits; it takes one into another's life, her hard times and, if there is any, her joy, too. There are women whose whole lives have been pornography and prostitution, and still they fight to live.

The world gets meaner as prostitution and pornography are legitimized. Now women are the slave population, an old slavery with a new technology, cameras and camcorders. Smile; say "bleed" instead of "cheese."

I'm tired, very weary, and I cry for my sisters. Tears get them nothing, of course. One needs a generation of warriors who can't be tired out or bought off. Each woman needs to take what she endures and turn it into action. With every tear, accompanying it, one needs a knife to rip a predator apart; with every wave of fatigue, one needs another platoon of strong, tough women coming up over the horizon to take more land, to make it safe for women. I'm willing to count the inches. The pimps and rapists need to be dispossessed, forced into a mangy exile; the women and children – the world's true orphans – need to be empowered, cosseted with respect and dignity.

Counting

Are there really women who have to worry about a fourth generation's becoming prostitutes? How many are there? Are there five, or 2,000, or 20 million? Are they in one place – for instance, the Pacific Northwest, where the woman I quoted lives – or are they in some sociological stratum that can be isolated and studied, or are they all in Thailand or the Philippines or Albania? Are there too many or too few, because in either case one need not feel responsible? Too many means it's too hard to do anything about it; too few means why bother. Is it possible that there is one adult woman in the United States who does not know whether or not a baby's body should be penetrated with an object, or are there so many that they cannot be counted – only their form of saying "I don't know" comes in the guise of labeling the penetration "speech" or "free speech"?

A few nights ago I heard the husband of a close friend on television discussing antirape policies that he opposes at a university. He said that he was willing to concede that rapes did take place. How white of you, I thought bitterly, and then I realized that his statement was a definition of "white" in motion – not even "white male" but white in a country built on white ownership of blacks and white genocide of reds and white-indentured servitude of Asians and women, including white women, and brown migrant labor. He thought that maybe 3 percent of women in the United States had been raped, whereas the best research shows a quarter to a third. The male interviewer agreed with this percentage pulled out of thin air: it sounded right to both of them, and neither of them felt required to fund a study or read the already existing research material. Their authority was behind their number, and in the United States authority is white. Whatever trouble these two particular men have had in their lives, neither has had to try to stop a fourth generation, their own child, from prostituting.

"I had two daughters from [him]," said a different woman, "and he introduced me into heroin and prostitution. I went further into drugs and prostitution, and all my life the only protection I ever had was my grandmother, and she died when I was five years old." This woman spoke about other males by whom she had children and was abused. She spoke about her mother, who beat her up and closed her in dark closets. It's good that her grandmother was kind because her grandfather wasn't: "I can't remember how old I was when my grandfather started molesting me, but he continued to rape me until I became pregnant at the age of thirteen." Can one count how many women there are on our fingers and toes, or does a bunch of us have to get together to have enough fingers and toes, or would it take a small army of women to get the right numbers?

There is another woman who was left in a garbage can when she was six months old. She was born drunk and had to be detoxified in her incubator. She was, in her own words, "partially mentally retarded," "abandoned," and "raised in and out of foster homes," some of which she says were good. She had the chance to stay with a foster family but chose to be with her father, since that was her idea of family. He was a brute, good with his fists, and first raped her when, as a child, she was taking a bath with her kid brother; and like many incest-rapists, he'd rape her or make her perform sex acts and then give her a child's reward. "I just wanted him to be my father; that's all I wanted from him," she said. At twelve she was stranger-raped. The stranger, a fairly talented pedophile, would pick her up from school and talk with her. Eventually he slammed her against a garage and raped her: "Nobody had ever talked to me about rape, so I figured he was just showing me love like my father did." On having the rape discovered, the girl was called no good, a whore, and shunned by her family. "My father had taught me most of what I needed to learn about pleasing men," she says. "There was a little bit more that [the pimp] needed to teach me. So [the pimp] would show me these videos, and I would copy on him what I saw was going on in the videos, and that's how I learned to be a prostitute." Her tricks were professional men. She worked in good hotels until she found herself streetwalking. "I ended up back in prostitution. I worked out on Fourth Street, which is the strip, and St. Carlos in San José. There were [many] times that I would get raped or beat up." Daddy pimped.

One night she was trying to bring home her quota of money when a drug-friend of her father's came by. "He raped me, he beat me up, he held a gun [in] his hand [to my head]. And I swear to this day I can still hear that gun clicking."

She then worries that she is taking up too much of my time. I'm important; she's not. My time matters; hers doesn't. My life matters; hers does not. From her point of view, from the reality of her experience, I embody wealth. I speak and some people listen. I write and one way or another the books get published from the United States and Great Britain to Japan and Korea. There is a splendidness to my seeming importance, especially because once parts of my life were a lot like parts of hers. How many of her are there? On my own I've counted quite a few.

These women are proud of me, and I don't want to let them down. I feel as if I've done nothing because I know that I haven't done enough. I haven't changed or destabilized the meaning of "white," nor could anyone alone. But writers write alone even in the context of a political movement. I've always seen my work as a purposeful series of provocations, especially *Pornography: Men Possessing Women*, *Ice and Fire*,

Intercourse, and *Mercy*. In other books I've devoted myself to the testimony of women who had no other voice. These books include *Letters from a War Zone*, currently being published in Croatia in its lonely trip around the world; the introduction to the second edition of *Pornography: Men Possessing Women*, which can also be found in *Life and Death: Writings on the Continuing War Against Women*, a collection of essays; and *In Harm's Way: The Pornography Civil Rights Hearings*, edited with Catharine A. MacKinnon and published by Harvard University Press. I still don't get to be white, because the people who care about what I say have no social importance.

I'm saying that white gets to say, "Yes, it happened" or "No, it didn't." I'm saying that there are always either too many or too few. I'm saying that I don't count sheep at night; I see in my mind instead the women I've met, I see their faces and I can recollect their voices, and I wish I knew what to do, and when people ask me why I'm such a hard-ass on pornography it's because pornography is the bible of sexual abuse; it is chapter and verse; pornography is the law on what you do to a woman when you want to have mean fun on her body and she's no one at all. No one does actually count her. She's at the bottom of the barrel. We're all still trying to tell the white guys that too many – not too few – women get raped. Rape is the screaming, burning, hideous top level of the rotten barrel, acid-burned damage, what you see if you look at the surface of violence against women. Rape plays a role in every form of sexual exploitation and abuse. Rape happens everywhere and it happens all the time and to females of all ages. Rape is inescapable for women. The act, the attempt, the threat – the three dynamics of a rape culture – touch 100 percent of us.

Heartbreak

How did I become who I am? I have a heart easily hurt. I believed that cruelty was most often caused by ignorance. I thought that if everybody knew, everything would be different. I was a silly child who believed in the revolution. I was torn to pieces by segregation and Vietnam. Apartheid broke my heart. Apartheid in Saudi Arabia still breaks my heart. I don't understand why every story about rising oil prices does not come with an addendum about the domestic imprisonment of women in the Gulf states. I can't be bought or intimidated because I'm already cut down the middle. I walk with women whispering in my ears. Every time I cry there's a name attached to each tear.

My ideology is simple and left: I believe in redistributing the wealth; everyone should have food and health care, shelter and safety; it's not right to hurt and deprive people so that they become prostitutes and thieves.

What I've learned is that women suffer from terrible shame and the shame comes from having been complicit in abuse because one wants to live. Middle-class women rarely understand how complicit they are unless they've experienced torture, usually in the home; prostituting women know that every breath is bought by turning oneself inside out so that the blood covers the skin; the skin is ripped; one watches the world like a hunted animal on all fours in the darkest part of every night.

There is nothing redemptive about pain.

Love requires an inner fragility that few women can afford. Women want to be loved, not to love, because to be loved requires nothing. Suppose that her love brought him into existence and without it he is nothing.

Men are shits and take pride in it.

Only the toughest among women will make the necessary next moves, the revolutionary moves, and among prostituted women one finds the toughest if not always the best. If prostituted women worked together to end male supremacy, it would end.

Surviving degradation is an ongoing process that gives you rights, honor, and knowledge because you earn them; but it also takes from you too much tenderness. One needs tenderness to love – not to be loved but to love.

I long to touch my sisters; I wish I could take away the pain; I've heard so much heartbreak among us. I think I've pretty much done what I can do; I'm empty; there's not much left, not inside me. I think that it's bad to give up, but maybe it's not bad to rest, to sit in silence for a while. I'm told by my friends that it's not evil to rest. At the same time, as they know, there's a child being pimped by her father with everyone around her either taking a piece of her or looking the other way. How can anyone rest, really? What would make it possible? I say to myself, Think about the fourth-generation daughter who wasn't a prostitute; think about her. I say, Think about the woman who asked herself whether or not it was bad to penetrate a baby with an object and figured out that it might be; think about her. These are miracles, political miracles, and there will be so many more. I think that there will be many more.

Basics

Politics doesn't run on miracles modest or divine, and the few miracles there are have the quality of invisibility about them because they happen to invisible people, those who have been hurt too much, too often, too deep. There's a jagged wound that is in fact someone's life, and any miracle is hidden precisely because the wound is so egregious. The victims of any systematized brutality are discounted because others cannot bear to see, identify, or articulate the pain. When a rapist stomps on your life, you are victimized, and although it is a social law in our society that "victim" is a dirty word, it is also a true word, a word that points one toward what one does not want to know.

Women used to be identified as a group by what was presumed to be a biological wound – the vaginal slit, the place for penile penetration. There is a 2,000 year history of the slit's defining the person. If a stranger can go from the outside to the inside, the instrumentality of that action is the whole purpose of the creature to whom it is done. That area of the female body has hundreds of dirty names that serve as synonyms.

The mystery is why the vagina is such a mystery. Any reference to one of the dirty names elicits sniggers and muted laughs. What are seen as the sexual parts of a woman's body are always jokes; anything nonsexual is trivial or trivialized.

For a prostitute, the whole body becomes the sexual part, as if there were nothing human, only an anatomical use. She gets to be dirty all over, and what is done to her gets to be dirty all over. She is also a joke. None of the women I've met in my life has been either dirty or a joke.

Feminists have good reasons for feeling tired. The backlash against feminism has been deeply stupid. But first there is the frontlash, the misogyny that saturates the gender system, so that a woman is always less. The frontlash is the world the way one knew it thirty-five years ago; there was no feminism to stand against the enemies of women.

I often see the women's movement referred to as one of the most successful social change movements the world has yet seen, and there is great truth in that. In some parts of the Western world, fathers do not own their daughters under the law; the fact that this has transmogrified into a commonplace incest doesn't change the accomplishment in rendering the paterfamilias a nullity in the old sense.

In most parts of the Western world, rape in marriage is now illegal – it was not illegal thirty-five years ago.

In the United States, most women have paying jobs, even though equal pay for equal work is a long way off; and although it is still true that sexual harassment makes women migrants in the labor market, the harassment itself is now illegal and one can sue – one has a weapon.

Middle-class women keep battery a secret and in working- and lower-class families battery is not sufficiently stigmatized; nevertheless, there are new initiatives against both battery and the batterer, and there will be more, including the nearly universal acceptance of a self-defense plea for killing a batterer.

The slime of woman hating comes now from the bottom, oozing its way up the social scale. There is a class beneath working and lower class that is entirely marginalized. It's the sex-for-money class, the whoring class, the pornography class, the trafficked-woman class, the woman who is invisible almost because one can see so much of her. Each inch of nakedness is an inch of worthlessness and lack of social protection. The world's economies have taken to trafficking in women; the woman with a few shekels is better off, they say, than the woman with none. I know a few formerly prostituted women, including myself, who disagree.

The women I've met are very often first raped, then pimped inside their own families while they are still children. Their bodies have no borders. Middle-class women, including middle-class feminists, cannot imagine such marginality. It's as if the story is too weird, too ugly, too unsightly for an educated woman to believe.

What comes along with every effort to stop the sexual abuse of women is the denial that the sexual abuse is happening at all, and U.S. women should understand that William Jefferson Clinton and his enabler, the senator, have set women back more than thirty-five years in this regard. Some women are pushed up and some women are pushed down. It's the women who are down who are paying the freight for all the rest; the women who have been pushed up even a smidge have taken to acting as if everything is all right or will be soon. Their arguments are not with men or even with subgroups of men, for instance, pimps. They smile and make nice with the men. Their arguments are with me or other militants. Being a militant simply requires fighting sexual abuse – the right of a rapist, the right of a pimp, the right of a john, the right of an incest-daddy to use or intimidate or coerce girls or women.

A young woman just out of college says that date rape does not happen, and the media conspire to make her rich and famous.

A woman of no intellectual distinction writes a 3,000-page book, or so it seems, and she is celebrated – she becomes rich and famous.

The wealthy wife of a multimillionaire writes longingly about being a stay-at-home mother. Feminists, she says, have made that too hard – as she pursues a golden career writing (without talent) about how she wants to be home mopping up infant vomit.

A middle-class English feminist of ferocious mediocrity spends her time charting the eating disorders of her betters.

They are not so evident on the landscape now, but there were so-called feminists who published in *Playboy*, *Hustler*, and *Penthouse* and penned direct attacks on feminists fighting pornography and prostitution. There were women labeled feminist who wrote pornographic scenarios in which the so-called fantasies were the rape of other feminists, usually named and sometimes drawn but always recognizable; one at least has become a male through surgery – her head and heart were always right there.

Making fun of the victims was even more commonplace than making fun of the feminists fighting in behalf of those who had been raped or prostituted.

It became an insult to be called or considered a victim, even when one had been victimized. The women in pornography and prostitution had not been victimized just once or by a stranger; more often the family tree was a poison tree – sexual abuse grew on every branch. Only in the United States could second-class citizens (women) be proud to disown the experiences of sisters (prostitutes), stand up for the predator, and minimize sexual abuse – this after thirty-five years spent fighting for the victim's right to live outside the dynamic of exploitation. "If you're ignorant to what's going on around you," said one former prostitute, "or haven't got the education to bring yourself out of that, you stay there. And so it becomes from the little go-go dancer to the strip-tease dancer to the glamorous effect to pornography, [and] coaxing other women into doing the same thing because I was a strong woman. Coming from a woman it sounds better, it comes across better, and I didn't realize I was doing it until I got the chance to do some healing. In the long run I was being tricked into it just like every other woman out there."

What does it mean if you call yourself a feminist, have the education, and act like a designer-special armed guard to keep women prostituting?

It is true, I think, that at the beginning, in the early years, feminists did not and could not imagine women hurting other women on purpose – being so morally or politically corrupt. The naïveté was stunning; betrayal is always an easier choice. One follows the patriarchal narrative by blaming the incest-mothers, the Chinese mothers who bound their daughters' feet, the bad mothers in the fairy tales. One did not want to follow the patriarchal narrative. But is it not the political responsibility of feminists to figure out the role of female-to-female betrayal in upholding male supremacy? Isn't that necessary? And how can one do what is necessary if one is too cowardly to face the truth?

The truth of a bad or incapacitated mother is a hard truth to face. As one woman said, "I was forced to be the head of the family because my mother couldn't do it. She was in a mental institution." Another woman said, "My mother was scared for men to be around [because] all my sisters were all molested by this man, and so she protected us from him, but a lady came in my life who seduced me and molested me also. I was twelve, and I thought I was safe." So there she was, the bad mother or the betraying mother or the incapacitated mother or the unknowing mother; and each had her own sadness or terror.

Not too many prostituting women got past twelve without being sexually abused, and not too many were childless, and not too many lived lives as teenagers and adults without men abusing them: "I was into drugs, in the limelights and the glamorous life, and thought I was better than the whores on the streets 'cause what I did was drove fancy cars and travel around in airplanes, all this shit, but I was still in the same pain as everybody else, [and] instead of using men I started using women for whatever my needs was." The media antifeminists are not unlike the woman-using prostitutes and the strung-out mothers – their venom goes in the direction of other women because it is easier than taking on men. Is this ever going to stop?

Immoral

People play life as if it's a game, whereas each step is a real step. The shock of being unable to control what happens, especially the tragedies, overwhelms one. Someone dies; someone leaves; someone lies. There is sickness, misery, loneliness, betrayal. One is alone not just at the end but all the time. One tries to camouflage pain and failure. One wants to believe that poverty can be cured by wealth, cruelty by kindness; but neither is true. The orphan is always an orphan.

The worst immorality is in apathy, a deadening of caring about others, not because they have some special claim but because they have no claim at all.

The worst immorality is in disinterest, indifference, so that the lone person in pain has no importance; one need not feel an urgency about rescuing the suffering person.

The worst immorality is in dressing up to go out in order not to have to think about those who are hungry, without shelter, without protection.

The worst immorality is in living a trivial life because one is afraid to face any other kind of life – a despairing life or an anguished life or a twisted and difficult life.

The worst immorality is in living a mediocre life, because kindness rises above mediocrity always, and not to be kind locks one into an ethos of boredom and stupidity.

The worst immorality is in imitating those who give nothing.

The worst immorality is in conforming so that one fits in, smart or fashionable, mock-heroic or the very best of the very same.

The worst immorality is accepting the status quo because one is afraid of gossip against oneself.

The worst immorality is in selling out simply because one is afraid.

The worst immorality is a studied ignorance, a purposeful refusal to see or know.

The worst immorality is living without ambition or work or pushing the rest of us along.

The worst immorality is being timid when there is no threat.

The worst immorality is refusing to push oneself where one is afraid to go.

The worst immorality is not to love actively.

The worst immorality is to close down because heartbreak has worn one down.

The worst immorality is to live according to rituals, rites of passage that are predetermined and impersonal.

The worst immorality is to deny someone else dignity.

The worst immorality is to give in, give up.

The worst immorality is to follow a road map of hate drawn by white supremacists and male supremacists.

The worst immorality is to use another person's body in the passing of time.

The worst immorality is to inflict pain.

The worst immorality is to be careless with another person's heart and soul.

The worst immorality is to be stupid, because it's easy.

The worst immorality is to repudiate one's own uniqueness in order to fit in.

The worst immorality is to set one's goals so low that one must crawl to meet them.

The worst immorality is to hurt children.

The worst immorality is to use one's strength to dominate or control.

The worst immorality is to surrender the essence of oneself for love or money.

The worst immorality is to believe in nothing, do nothing, achieve nothing.

The worst immoralities are but one, a single sin of human nothingness and stupidity. "Do no harm" is the counterpoint to apathy, indifference, and passive aggression; it is the fundamental moral imperative. "Do no harm" is the opposite of immoral. One must do something and at the same time do no harm. "Do no harm" remains the hardest ethic.

Memory

Memory became political on the global scale when Holocaust survivors had to remember in order to testify against Nazi war criminals. It had always been political to articulate a crime that had happened to one and name the criminal, but that had been on a small scale: the family, the village, the local legal system. Sometimes one remembered but made no accusation. This was true with pogroms as well as rapes.

There have been Holocaust survivors who refused to remember, and there is at least one known Holocaust survivor who is a Holocaust denier.

It has been hard to get crimes against women recognized as such. Rape was a crime against the father or husband, not the victim herself. Incest was a privately protected right hidden under the imperial robe of the patriarch. Prostitution was a crime in which the prostitute was the criminal no matter who forced her, who hurt her, or how young she was in those first days of rape without complicity. A woman's memory was so inconsequential that her word under oath meant nothing.

Now we have a kind of half-memory; one can remember being raped, but remembering the name and face of the rapist, saying the name aloud, pointing to the face, actually compromises the victim's claim. People are willing to cluck empathetically over the horror of rape as long as they are not made responsible for punishing the rapist.

Proust's madeleine signifies the kind of memory one may have. That memory may be baroque. A regular woman who has been coerced had better have a very simple story to tell and a rapist dripping with gold lamé guilt instead of sweat.

A worker in a rape crisis center told me this story. It happened down the street from where I live. A woman moved into a new apartment on the parlor level, slightly elevated from the street but not by much. She needed to have someone come into her new apartment to install new windows. The worker did most of the work but said that he needed a particular tool in order to finish. He said that he would be willing to come back that evening to finish the job. The woman was grateful; after all, there is nothing quite as dangerously insecure as an urban apartment near the ground floor with unlocked windows. He came back; he beat and raped her. At the trial his defense was that he had been her boyfriend, she had had sex with him many times, she liked it rough, and as with the other times this was not rape. She, of course, did not know him at all.

The jury believed him, which is to say that they had reasonable doubt about her testimony. After all, she could not prove that he had not been her boyfriend, that she had never met him before that day. This scenario has to be the world's worst rape nightmare outside the context of torture and mass murder. It was so simple for him.

The point is that once the victim can identify the predator, once she says his name and goes to court, there is no empathy for her, not on the part of all the good, civic-minded citizens on the jury, not from the media reporting on the case (if they do), not from men and women socializing in bars. She's got the mark of Cain on her; he does not. All the sympathy tilts toward him, and he has an unchangeable kind of credibility with which he was born. To ruin his life with a charge of rape is heinous – more heinous than the rape. No matter how many rapists go free, the society does not change the way the scales of justice are weighted; he's got a pound of gold by virtue of being a male, and she's got a pound of feathers. It couldn't be more equal.

People deal with hideous events in different ways, and one way is to forget them. A forgotten event is not always sexual or abusive. I worked very hard for years as a writer and feminist. One night I had dinner with a distant cousin. "I remember when you used to play the piano," she said. I didn't remember that fact of my life at all and had not for decades. My life had changed so much, I had so little use for the memory, perhaps, that I had forgotten the years of piano lessons and recitals. I sat stunned. She was bewildered. She insisted: "Don't you remember?" I was blank until she gave me some details. Then

I began to remember. In fact, she had remembered my life as a pianist over a period of decades during which I had forgotten it.

With sexual abuse, people remember and people forget. The process of remembering can be slow, tormenting, sometimes impossible. Aharon Appelfeld thanks the Holocaust survivors who insisted on remembering when all he wanted to do was forget. There are at least two Holocaust memoirs about forgetting, and if one can forget a concentration camp one can forget a rape. If one can forget as an adult, a child can surely forget.

I read some years ago about a study in which a mother chimpanzee was fitted with a harness that had knives sticking out; her babies were released into her presence; trying to embrace her they were cut; the more cut they were the more they tried to hold tight to her; the more they were hurt the more they wanted their mother. The research itself is repugnant, but the terrifying story of what happened during it strikes me as an accurate parable of a child's love, blind love, and desperate need. Remembering and forgetting are aspects of needing and loving, not rulers of what the heart does or does not know. Those who say children are lying when they remember as adults abuse they endured as children are foolish – as are those who think children categorically do not know when they've been hurt.

I remember a lot of things that happened in my life. Sometimes I wish I remembered every little thing. Sometimes

I think that the best gift on dying would be if God gave one that second between life and death in which to know everything all at once, all that one ever wanted to know. For myself, I'd include every fact of my own experience but especially the earliest years – and I'd like to know everything about my parents, what they thought and what they dreamed. I'd like to know our lineage all the way back, who my ancestors were and what made them tick. I have a few questions about lovers and friends, too. At the same time I want to know the truth about the cell, the galaxy, the universe, where it began and how it will end. I'd like to know what the sun is really like – it's not just fire and cold spots – as much as I'd like to know how there can be so much empty space inside a molecule. I'd like to go back and redo my high school physics class and really master the language of mathematics. I'd like to know if there is a God and what faith means. I'd like to know how Shakespeare wrote from the inside out. I know that if there are black holes in the universe, multiple personalities simply cannot be impossible. In fact they have God's mark all over them as an elegant solution to a vile problem – children forced to live in hell find ways to chop the hell up, a child becomes plural, and each part of the plurality must handle some aspect of the hell as if it's got all of it. This is more complicated than fragmenting a personality, but there is nothing difficult to understand. The child becomes many children, and each has a personality and work cut out for it; each personality helps the child endure. What is difficult is how children are hurt, and sometimes the denial of multiple personalities, which is, of course, a denial of memory, is also a denial of sexual abuse. The story isn't simple enough to be believed by outsiders, but the victim has found a way to survive. It's miraculous, really. One ritual-abuse survivor with double-digit personalities told me to think of her as a small army fighting for the rights of women. I do.

A memoir, which this is, says: this is what my memory insists on; this is what my memory will not let go; these points of memory make me who I am, and all that others find incomprehensible about me is explained by what's in here. I need to say that I don't care about being understood; I want my work to exist on its merits and not on the power of personality or celebrity. I have done this book because a lot of people asked me to, and I hope this work can serve as a kind of bridge over which some girls and women can pass into their own feminist work, perhaps more ambitious than mine but never less ambitious, because that is too easy. I want women to stop crimes against women. There I stand or fall.

Acknowledgments

This book owes everything to Elaine Markson. She wanted me to write it and helped me at every step along the way.

I also want to thank Nikki Craft, Sally Owen, Eva Dworkin, Michael Moorcock, Linda Moorcock, Robin Morgan, John Stoltenberg, Susan Hunter, Jane Manning, Sheri DiPelesi, Louise Armstrong, Julie Bindell, Gail Abarbanel, Valerie Harper, and Gretchen Langheld for their support.

I am grateful to David Evans, producer for the BBC1 series *Omnibus*. I used testimony from the documentary done on my work by David; he helped make the last third of this book possible.

I am also grateful to my editor, Elizabeth Maguire, for her useful suggestions and great enthusiasm. I thank her assistant, William Morrison, and all the other folks at Basic Books for their work in publishing *Heartbreak*.